Alternatives to Society's Taboos

– BILL WATSON –

An environmentally friendly book printed and bound in England by

www.printondemand-worldwide.com

Mixed Sources
Product group from well-managed
forests, and other controlled sources
www.fsc.org Cert no. TT-COC-002641
© 1996 Forest Stewardship Council

FSC

PEFC Certified
This product is
from sustainably
managed forests
and controlled
sources

PEFC
PEFC/16-33-415

www.pefc.org

This book is made entirely of chain-of-custody materials

www.fast-print.net/store.php

ALTERNATIVES TO SOCIETY'S TABOOS
Copyright © Bill Watson 2013

A catalogue record for this book is available from the British Library

ISBN 978-178035-721-8

First published 2013 by
FASTPRINT PUBLISHING
Peterborough, England.

Acknowledgments

I would like to thank my wife Kath who is a veritable walking dictionary and custodian of the English Language. Unlike myself who would like to see it reformed, starting with the confusing and archaic spelling.

Finally I would like to thank Mr Ian Spittle my IT man. He has been my IT man through the last three books that I have published. Without him I might have given up without publishing anything.

CONTENTS

Introduction

It was August in 2011 when riots broke out in the UK. They started in London and then spread to provincial cities including Wolverhampton. I was sitting in a garden outside a working men's club when someone asked for an explanation of what had gone wrong. I had been following the situation closely right from the inception and I gave my views and explanations of what had gone wrong, and how it could be solved in the long run. There was quite a long list of taboo subjects included in my reply but no one disagreed with what I had to say.

The next morning I got up early as usual and started this book. I first concentrated on the riots but this led on to other things. I realised that there are a number of taboo subjects and tried to offer alternatives.

I have noticed a tendency for leading politicians to waffle around a question without saying anything. If they do not have an answer to the question, they should say so. They should not be afraid to change their minds about issues which have been around for a long time. Why not simply be honest and say you have changed your mind since the issue first arose.

While researching this book I have changed my mind about many things. One is the minimum wage which I have included in my chapter on Economics. I have always supported a minimum wage, until I realised that this could be a disincentive to work unless it offered well above the minimum. If someone needs a basic income I have called it a National Living Allowance. Everyone needs it and should get it irrespective of whether they receive current benefit from pensions or the dole. **This should include those working**. With a National Living Allowance it is then worthwhile for someone to take a job with as little at £40 pounds a week.

I changed my mind several times in my chapter on The Animal World, but not my love of animals which has been with me since childhood. I was sickened by the way rhinos are treated in the wild. But I finally came up with the idea of farming the rhinos which would bring down the price and take pressure off the few wild ones left. I did have a precedent for this one. I had carefully studied the farming of the Bengal tigers in Sriracha zoo in Thailand. Many of them finish up in China for

Chinese medicine which takes some of the pressure off those that remain in the wild and might otherwise be hunted to extinction.

In my final chapter on Defence & War I concentrated on the nuclear deterrent. I could see only one use for it – Argentina. In a future Falkland's war there would be no option, give in or threaten to use nuclear weapons. My solution is certainly a taboo subject but it could save the tax payer billions of pounds.

Alternatives to Society's Taboos

BILL WATSON

THE POPULATION CRISIS

In November 2011 the world population reached 7 billion. I watched in horror as the media *celebrated this event* with their predictable attempt to try and personalise it with a search for the child who completed the 'magic number'. A lot of nonsense really; we do not even have an accurate figure for the UK population and for many others countries the numbers must be very rough estimates.

Sir David Attenborough

Sir David Attenborough has educated and entertained us for many years. In 2013 he was eighty six and still making his documentaries. I watched one last night (13/07/2013); it was about a giant squid off the coast of Japan. As age takes its toll he is less and less active in his documentaries but still he has a role to play and will continue to work as long as he is able to do so.

I have noticed over the past few years his increasing concern over the planet we live on and how there are fewer and fewer natural habitats for wildlife. After watching one of his wildlife programs I often think that he should 'come out' to the obvious cause – human beings. Then I think that he would not last very long if he made such 'politically incorrect conclusions' and left the viewers to make up their own minds.

Then at last he 'came out' earlier this year to give his opinions on the world population.

Sir David Attenborough's Views

He has warned that human beings have become a "plague on the Earth".

"The negative effects of climate change and population growth would be seen over the next 50 years. It's coming home to roost over the next 50 years or so."

"It's not just climate change; it's sheer space, places to grow food for this enormous horde."

"Either we limit our population growth or the natural world will do it for us, and the natural world is doing it for us right now."

My Views

David Attenborough's views are something he has held for some time and it is incredible that he has now 'come out'. The expanding world population is a continuing theme of this book. Being a nobody I have nothing to lose by expressing my views; although they will be 'politically incorrect', very hard at times (famines) but the reader can judge for themselves.

I have never thought that the life of a tiger or rhino is worth less than the life of a single human being. The animals are an endangered species; humans are not.

Famines

A dictionary definition of famine is very simple: a severe shortage of food which leads to starvation.

The word has Latin roots and passed through the old French before becoming an everyday word of which most people have a basic understanding.. Of course there must have been words for it in many different languages long before Roman times because famines have been a part of the history of man since the very beginning.

In the days of the hunter-gatherer, communities were very small; famines might have been quite local and would often result in the death of the whole community. With the advent of agriculture the size of communities increased at an astonishing rate. The human population increased dramatically. Famines were caused by loss of farmed animals or crop failures, the latter being by far the most important. Crops can fail due to attacks by disease or insects or simply lack of water.

Whatever the cause of the crop failure it would be likely to affect a much larger area. If starvation and death resulted, many more people would be lost than would be the case in pre-agricultural communities but the percentage might be much smaller. It is very unlikely that everyone would die. The most likely to die would be the very young and the very old – the weakest members of the community.

Famines played a major role in the development of mankind. There is also no doubt that historically the human population in the area after a famine would be significantly lower than it had been before the famine. They were a driving force in the process of natural selection –

the 'survival of the fittest'. There was also a side benefit due to the migration of people away from the area affected, thus spreading their gene pool.

As communities developed into states and countries new factors arose. This affected how famines could be dealt with – by means of distribution of aid and political motivation.

The classic example of the latter failing badly is the Great Famine in Ireland between 1846 and 1849. The basic diet of most of the population was the humble potato. Their potato crop was attacked by the blight in successive years. At the time Ireland was also producing a lot of cattle and cereal crops but most of these were exported – mainly to England. Throughout the famine Ireland was a net exporter of food. There was no famine in the rest of the British Isles.

The result of the famine was one of the greatest reductions of population in recent history. About one million people died due to starvation or the diseases which follow malnutrition and another two million emigrated – mainly to America, England or Australia. The total population was halved and continued to decline until the 1970's.

The people who emigrated eventually fared much better that the ones that remained and there are now over fifteen times as many people of Irish descent in other countries as there are living in Ireland today.

Today's famines

Famines are still with us today. They are concentrated in the Northern Hemisphere of Africa particularly the horn. There are some too in Bangladesh and Burma during the monsoon season when they have their floods which seem to be getting worse.

One thing I have noticed is that unlike the famines of the past there is no noticeable decrease in the population. The population continues to explode and they are among the worst examples of a population explosion.

In Africa the cause is normally repeated crop failures when the rains never come as expected. They soon have to use up their precious seed grain that they needed for the next crop, resulting in a famine.

The Ethiopian famine in the mid 1980's is something the reader will be familiar with. Bob Geldof raised money in 1985 with "Do they know it's Christmas?" The familiar Red Nose Day was born and continues to be an annual event.

Since then there have been many Ethiopian famine appeals until the present day. The political situation does not help and many cargos designed as famine relief are hijacked to feed the militants. But the population continues to grow. The media with its band of photographic images continue to get the best shots for mass media coverage. They get very well paid for this. Their ideal shot is one of the worst cases of a child suffering malnutrition with the caption that "a mother of six who has already lost two children to malnutrition" is ideal.

If aid reaches her, the first thing she will do is to replace the children which she lost. It is a heart-rending situation but I cannot help wondering if the first famine should have been left to its own inevitable course.

Disease

During the First World War it is estimated that about 16 million people lost their lives. Just afterwards there was an influenza epidemic which eventually killed an estimated 60 million people. About one fifth of the world's population was attacked by this deadly virus.

It started in the late spring of 1918 when it became known as "three-day fever". Few deaths were reported at first and the victims recovered after a few days. When the disease surfaced again it was far more severe. The soldiers gave it the name "Spanish Flu" but there is no evidence that it originated there. The first recorded case was in Glasgow in May 1918 and in the next few months there were 228,000 people dead in Britain.

By comparison there are 887,000 soldiers from the UK and its colonies listed as dead in WW1 and 1,600,000 were wounded.

The Spanish Flu was not easily recognisable by doctors and scientists and they never found a cure. Some patients developed a bluish colouration and were easy to spot and died in the first few days. Others developed bronchial pneumonia after developing a fever.

It is difficult to know how many casualties of WW1 in 1918 could be put down to the Spanish Flu. An American hospital on the Western Front in 1918 had 70,000 patients and a third of them died from the Spanish Flu. The wounded were taken back to America. It soon spread from the East Coast of America all the way up to Alaska and by the time it had finished 450,000 had died of Spanish Flu in the US. The life expectancy suddenly dropped by about 12% in a year. In Germany about 400,000 civilians died.

India was the worst region hit and it was first reported in Bombay in June 1918. There were large numbers of Indian doctors involved in British hospitals and the usual wounded. The flu quickly spread to Karachi and Madras and it ended with over 16,000,000 dead of the virus. Over the world it is estimated that 60 million people died of Spanish Flu.

In the UK it is not the highest mortality rate recorded from a disease; there were certainly more deaths (per head of population) in the plague of 1665. The "Black Death" as it is commonly known is bubonic plague which had been around Europe since 1347 and lasted until 1750. It started in London again when the Great Fire of London broke out. The fleeing citizens who had lost their homes soon spread across the county and many took the plague with them. In London alone there were reported to be 100,000 deaths from the plague and elsewhere in the country as a whole there were about 200,000 deaths.

In 1849 there was a cholera epidemic in the UK. It is difficult to get figures for this one. I found some very detailed analysis for London where 7,466 died but then another quoted around 13,000. In the UK there were probably over 33,000 died. Most of the deaths centred on sea ports. Cholera is now curable and there were no cases for a long time but recently there are some cases due to our mix of population and long distance travel. These affect only a few people (probable less than 100) but elsewhere in the word it is still a killer particularly in displaced communities where there is lack of sanitation and they do not have the medicine at hand to cure it.

During the writing of this section I was repeatedly confused with the definition of epidemic and pandemic. My dictionary definition of epidemic is a disease which is limited to a region or part of a country. For pandemic it is a disease which affects more than one country. A lot of the research above refers to epidemic when clearly it a case of pandemic (by today's definition). Now everything seems to be pandemic no matter how many people are involved?

Today

Today, neither famine, war nor disease helps us to reduce the world's exploding population. I once heard a sick comment by a white South African that their exploding population (mainly black) would be settled by Aids.

In the developed world we have now a plethora of medicines available to us. Antibiotics are an important example of these. Repeated use of antibiotics can lead to antibiotic resistance. In Europe there is a European Antibiotics Awareness Day which is held annually on November 18th. There are variants of flu and each one requires an individual treatment which can be added to the general flu vaccine. I have no doubt that our scientists can keep on top of this. In the underdeveloped world it takes time for the pharmaceutical companies who developed the drugs to come to the conclusion that some people cannot afford them. In conclusion I doubt if any disease in future will make an impact on population.

We just have to do it ourselves with a very serious planning program of birth control.

Many European countries have done it with their 'indigenous populations', Germany and the UK are some who have. In the UK we have an unfortunate system of planning where the government allow breeding from the underclass (who cannot and in some cases do not want to get a job) and the successful classes who go on to university despite the punitive costs of paying for it without any grants and will emerge with £30,000 debts for their efforts. By the time they have got on to the housing ladder they will have typically only one or two children (see chapter on eugenics for more details).

Of course the populations have not gone down in Europe and they are set to increase. This is due to immigration from around the world in quite recent times. (Those who have been born in this country and are now reaching the stage of adulthood are not responsible for our population explosion.)

The Pope

The Catholic Church has spread ignorance and hope (to see a better life after this one) throughout history. It is now no longer important in terms of population explosion in Europe, where I would describe many as 'selective Catholics' who tend to ignore the Church's policy on birth control. Elsewhere it is a serious matter where they continue to spread ignorance and hope in equal measures. There it is a serious barrier to limiting the population explosion.

In Europe they are on safer grounds with their call for a 'sanctity of life' appeal. Once an egg had been fertilised the sanctity of life applies to their assessment. It does not matter how the child is conceived; a multiple rape of the mother is an extreme example. A more common example is the situation where the life of the mother is in serious danger if she continues with the pregnancy. The difference between a mother's right to demand an abortion and no right at all is a continuing issue which affects not only the Catholic Church. I would maintain that even in the late stages of pregnancy, if the child is known to inherit a deformity, it is not too late to terminate it.

The Muslims

These are one of the fastest growing religions worldwide and many of them see it as a means of propagating their religious ideal by having a ban on birth control. This affects the UK and all those who have substantial Muslim communities. There are more details of this in my chapter on Religion.

A Shining Example

China had set a shining example of how to treat the world's population explosion. It decided to do this in 1978. It restricts many couples to one child only; exceptions to this are twins, rural couples, couples who are both only children themselves and certain ethnic minorities. In 2007 a committee spokesman on the One-Child Policy said that about 36% of the population was subject to the policy. He estimated that this had prevented more than 250 million births between 1980 and 2000.

I can personally back up some of the statistics, when I was working with a Chinese colleague in Thailand between spring and early summer of 2006. She was a graduate, in her mid-twenties and she had been brought up in Shanghai. She was a very thoughtful young lady but did not hesitate when I queried about the One-Child policy in China. "It is just something we accept as the norm; all my colleagues at school and university are the same." We discussed the world population in general and she seemed to be very knowledgable about what was going on in the outside world.

Some doubt the figures I have quoted above but they are nit-picking about figures issued by a 'committee spokesman'. The urban population is still growing at the expense of the rural communities so that today more and more people will be will be subject to the One-Child policy.

Today rural communities are coming in to line with birth control although this depends on local jurisdiction. The media in general in this country concentrate on 'hard luck' stories about people who have infringed party policy. They talk about the 'infringement of human rights'. What they should be talking about is China's policy as a whole in stabilising the world population explosion.

An example of family planning which has failed

India it top of this list. It is a never-ending argument about population control. Some wish to limit some areas of the population but not others. They have a higher Muslim population than in Pakistan who will have none of it.

The most populous nations are still China with about 19% closely followed by India with 17% according to the census in 2011. India will soon overtake China as being the most populous nation on earth.

.India still has family advice for limiting the population in some States but female foeticide remains common. Sons are still seen as wage earners of the future. The literacy rate has improved but it still stands at about 26%. Education is a key issue for family planning.

There are many other examples of introducing family planning throughout the world but they have had limited success.

EUGENICS

For decades now we have had benefit and social housing policies that have encouraged the least well off members of our society to have the most children. The more incapable they are at making a contribution to society the more children they are likely to have.

Convicted criminals have demanded conjugal rights to produce more criminals when society should be offering them reduced sentences in return for voluntary sterilisation.

The underclasses rioting in August 2011 were so used to free hand outs that they saw looting as just another social benefit they were entitled to. Advertising fuelled their desire for consumer goods that they could not afford but thought they must have.

Politicians and community leaders pleaded with the parents of the young people involved in the riots to keep their children at home; some were more likely to give them a 'shopping list' or join them. Many of the parents involved were not fit to keep a pet and should not be bringing up children.

Hazel Blears the MP for Salford and Eccles, a former Labour cabinet minister – 'Secretary of State for Communities and Local Government 2007-9'asked the question "why were the children not at school?" when it was in the middle of the school holidays. Most MPs and other community leaders responded with less obvious gaffes and comments about the police etc.

At the other end of the social scale the most successful and responsible young people have been having fewer children. I first became aware of this trend in the late nineteen seventies. I was working as a lecturer at what is now Wolverhampton University and I knew how many children many fellow members of staff had. During the same period I spent a lot of my social life playing darts in the evening. I was quite good and won many local competitions without ever quite managing to get into the county team. (The West Midlands was a very strong team at that time.) My job and my social life meant that I was in regular contact with a wide social mix of people. I noticed that the people I met who were on benefits (although many did 'work on the side') were likely to have the largest families.

At the same time as the riots were taking place, a new generation of our most successful young people were facing such an exorbitant increase in higher education tuition fees that some were deciding to forget higher education because they could not face the estimated £50,000 debts they would have to repay at the end of it. Those who do carry on are likely to postpone having a family until they have cleared the debts. Consequently they are likely to have even fewer children than they might otherwise have done.

I wrote my usual spate of letters to the media pointing out that any long term solutions must include a rethink of our crazy eugenic policies. Of course it was too much of a taboo subject for any of them to risk publishing it.

A Basic Definition

A simple definition is as follows:

"Eugenics is the study of the methods of improving the quality of the human race."

This definition is very simple and if strictly adhered to it would mean that I should have been using the term 'anti-eugenic' to describe government policies since they clearly have a policy of worsening the quality of the human race by encouraging the least successful to have children while discouraging the most successful.

However, man is only a single species of the animal world which share this planet and it is useful to look at what has happened to other animals in a very short period of time in evolutionary terms.

A Comparison with Animals

If anyone said to a racehorse breeder that, after their stock had proved to be winners or been found wanting on the track, they should breed most of the new generation from those which had never won a race, they would quite rightly assume that anyone proposing such an idea was stupid.

Mankind has been selectively breeding animals since they first started to domesticate them. This was not Darwinism of course; there was nothing 'natural' about the selective processes used. They simply wanted sheep that would produce more meat or wool; cattle that would produce more meat or milk and horses that would be swifter to carry communications between settlements and in battle, or be more efficient at pulling a plough. The conflicting requirement for horses meant that totally different looking animals were bred.

The diversity in animals has been taken to extreme limits in the case of domesticated dogs. They were needed to pull sledges, guard settlements and hunt a variety of wild animals from the noble stag to vermin such as rats. Different breeds were developed for each type of prey. The German Shepherd is still used to round up cattle and any everyone will be familiar with the lovable Collie used to round up sheep since it added to our passive entertainment in televised competitions.

However in parallel with the development of working dogs was the development of dogs as pets and fashion accessories. Some of these developments were sensible and reasonable but far too many were not. Breeds have been developed with such short legs that they can barely walk; others with such flat faces that they have breathing problems. The magnificent German Shepherd dog has even been selectively bred to have a round back which resulted in severe hip problems. In the UK the culprits responsible for these abominations were the governing body of the British Kennel Club but I expect that similar organisations in other countries have made their own mistakes. (There is an account of me watching real German Shepherd dogs at work in my book –'A different view of the Camino de Santiago.')

One of the most interesting developments in dogs is the Pit Bull Terrier. They are certainly very aggressive dogs and potentially very dangerous. Unfortunately they seem to have become a status symbol for some of the undesirable members of our society and, even worse, they are still used as fighting dogs. A lot of money can change hands during such clandestine fights which take place in temporary 'pits'. However the name predates any fighting. They were developed to be working dogs to work in the other type of pit – the mine. They were used to haul coal and minerals through tunnels that were too low to accommodate a pit pony. (It is not too long ago that ponies were used in the UK – I remember seeing some in the early nineteen sixties by a mine in Durham.)

Genetic Techniques

In recent years advances in the understanding of DNA has led to completely new branches of science of which, for once, the general public are very aware.This of course is due to the excellent science fiction film Jurassic Park. Like all the best science fiction it was based on an idea which is theoretically possible. The idea was then developed into a fantasy world by integrating the latest animation technology with conventional filming and personal stories of the people involved.

However genetic science is not just the basis of fantasy worlds for our entertainment. It is already confronting society with issues which must be faced now.

Genetically Modified (GM) crops are already a reality and a controversial issue. Modifying the DNA of a high yield crop by adding a gene from a disease resistant variety clearly has advantages over spraying with chemicals several times a year, but what if the DNA is passed on to weeds which might become rampant?

GM crops are now legally grown in many countries of the world including the USA. In the UK they are in the experimental stage but not part of our general agricultural options. Of course a GM modified cereal is not necessarily used to produce a loaf of bread – it may just be used as an animal feed. One way or another I suspect that most of us have ingested food with an ingredient which contains a GM-modified product somewhere down the line.

GM modified animals are still in the experimental stage as far as I know. One interesting development is GM-modified pigs. Their DNA is a very close match with that of humans, and pigs may one day provide body parts such as hearts and livers – very good news for all the people who die each year because of lack of organ donors.

I think that we need to keep a very open mind on all these developments as we should about basic eugenics.

A History of Eugenics

The word "eugenics" was invented by Sir Francis Galton in 1883 when he published his book 'Inquiries into human faculty and its development'. He was born near Sparkbrook in Birmingham and educated at King Edward's School in Birmingham, Cambridge University and other institutions. A strong influence on his pre-school years was his elder sister, Adele, who had a spinal injury and spent most of her time in bed. She taught him to read and write at a very early age before he started school at the age of five.

Galton was a genius who contributed to many fields of knowledge including mathematics, metrology, exploration and anthropology. The first ever weather map which appeared in The Times in 1875 was his map. He was the originator of modern fingerprinting techniques in forensic science.

He had published books and technical papers on a variety of scientific topics and was already a fellow of the Royal Geographical Society and the Royal Society before he turned to eugenics. Like his second cousin Charles Darwin, he meticulously collected all the statistical data he could before publishing late in life, knowing he lived in an age were only an enlightened minority had accepted his cousin's theories of evolution.

After publishing his book he founded a eugenics society and when he died in 1911 he left part of his wealth to fund a chair of Eugenics in the University of London.

The British Eugenics Society became a well established scientific group. Some well known members included Winston Churchill, H G Wells, George Bernard Shaw, Sidney Webb and Marie Stopes.

On the other side of the Atlantic in the USA, eugenic concepts were supported by Theodore Roosevelt, J H Kellogg, Linus Pauling, Margaret Sanger and Alexander Graham Bell. (The latter carried out detailed research on the congenitally deaf and came to the conclusion that an offspring from a couple who were both afflicted had a very high chance of producing a child with the same problem. He simply advised such couples not to marry.)

Government applications of eugenic policies in the USA are difficult to summarize because of the complexity of differences between state and federal laws. Indiana was the first state to pass a sterilization bill in 1907. Oregon performed the last legal 'forced' sterilization in U.S. history in 1981. A figure of 60,000 Americans being 'forcibly' sterilised is widely quoted. Such a relatively low figure could not include 'voluntary' cases. The mentally retarded who were incapable of looking after themselves were the sole target.

The Nixon administration (1968-1974) increased Medicaid funds for 'voluntary' sterilization. These targeted the poor, for whom it was a birth control option, as well as the mentally retarded.

Sweden

Sweden is a more straightforward example of a eugenic law. Their Sterilization Act of 1934 provided for the voluntary sterilization of some mental patients. The law was supported by all the political parties of the day as well as by their medical profession and the Lutheran Church.

Between 1934 and 1975 62,000 mentally ill people were involved. Other Scandinavian countries passed similar laws and per head of population Finland had a higher figure.

In recent years most of what has been written about the eugenic policies of the above countries has been damning. It is often by people and organizations which are predictably biased. They have carefully sought out and emphasized any example of misuse and abuse they could find. I have read through a plethora of data on the Internet without finding any positive statements. A lot of the comments of course are built around the definition of what is 'voluntary' and what is 'forced', in many articles the former is frequently assumed to be the latter.

Michael Johnson's "speed gene" theory

Michael Johnson who won gold medals in the 200 m and 400 m in the 1996 Olympics is now one of the most knowledgeable and thoughtful sporting commentators in the media. He has an explanation for the dominance of 'black' athletes from the American continent in general and the tiny country of Jamaica in particular in present day sprinting events. He presented his ideas in a TV program in July 2012.

He acknowledged that he was not the first personality to suggest what he had to say. In 1988 a US media man, Jimmy Snyder said that black athletes were superior because they had been "bred to be that way". His remark was quickly condemned by all those people in power who react without any in-depth analysis and he lost what had been a very good job.

Twenty four years later attitudes may have become a little more tolerant but it is much more difficult to dismiss the same idea as racist when it is proposed by a 'black'. I have deliberately used quotation marks around the term 'black' up to now because hardly any of the people we are discussing are genetically 100% Negroid. Michael Johnston's own genetic code is 90% Negroid which consist of genes from several distinct groups in the west coast of Africa where the majority of slaves came from.

This mix of African genes, Johnson suggests, may be one of the factors which influenced the final product but his main case is based on the harsh realities of the slave trade. Slaves were taken from areas which were often remote from the coast and were forced to walk hundreds of miles to the pounds in the coastal forts were they were sorted and sold for the second time to the ship owners who transported them across the Atlantic. The weaker ones died before they reached the coast.

The transporter ships were specially designed to cram in as many slaves as possible and if the crossing took longer than expected they would be running out of food and water. Consequently many more died during the crossing – only the strongest and fittest reached the new world. Once there, they would be sold again to the plantation owners from the Caribbean islands and the Southern States of America.

Once on a plantation they were treated like any livestock would be on farms. The strongest and fittest males were selected to breed with the females to produce the strongest and fittest children who would grow up to spend their lives toiling in the fields. This was intentional eugenics not the 'accidental' eugenics associated with the original transportation.

Jamaica had a special role in the slave trade because it was often the first landing place after the Atlantic crossing. It had its own sugar plantations which required slaves but it was also used as a place where slaves would be 'fattened up' and given time to recover from the crossing so that they would bring higher prices at the auctions. Once the slaves had recovered their strength they were in a better position to consider an escape. Some of the stronger and most ingenious ones did and slave revolts became a feature of the island's history – another tier of selection.

One of the few points which Johnson made with which I would take issue concerns aggression. He deliberately introduced the topic but only to say that aggression was not an issue. It is well established that, not only did plantation owners have selective breeding programs to produce efficient workers; some would also have their own fighters and match them against fighters from other plantations. Two blacks fighting in front of a mainly white audience, who would pay good money to watch, and wager a lot more money on the outcome, were a feature of the times. I have often reflected on how often this has been repeated in more recent times in a professional boxing ring.

It only took a relatively small number of generations to produce Michael Johnson's 'fastest and fittest' through slavery and the most compelling evidence that it did is that there are hardly any sprinters from the countries where the slaves originally came from.

Jesse Owens' Story

At the infamous Berlin Olympic Games in 1936 Hitler wanted a world platform to demonstrate the superiority of the Arian race in general and the prowess of German athletes under his form of government in particular.

His dreams were shattered by the performance of the black USA athletes in the field and track events. Those games are often referred to as the Jesse Owens games because he won four gold medals. Clearly many of the German athletes taking part did not share their Fuhrer's views on race. Luz Long who was narrowly beaten by Owens in the long jump warmly congratulated his rival.

When Owens was interviewed by the press about Hitler's beliefs and attitude to black athletes he made the very interesting comment "Hitler didn't snub me, it was FDR (Franklin D Roosevelt) who snubbed me. The President didn't even send me a telegram."

There is no doubt that the UK government's current eugenics policy is unintentional but we already have three or four generations of families who have never worked and yet they are producing more children than society's most successful families – why?

Germany

Events in Germany during the Nazi party period of power – the Third Reich - seem to have ended sensible debates on eugenics in the UK when they seemed to be merged and confused with racialism and genocide which should be treated as quite separate issues.

Racialist and genocidal policies have been around since the beginning of recorded time. Any reader who doubts this does not need to go back too far in history - the USA, Australia and New Zealand all have examples of both. The most recent examples are mainly in Africa; The Congo, Nigeria, Kenya and worst of all Rwanda. Outside Africa the current Sri Lankan government is now being accused of genocide against its Tamil population.

Only the events in Rwanda could reasonably be compared with the holocaust in Germany in terms of the numbers involved and the methods used. The holocaust will always be a prime example of the depths to which human beings can sink and the simple way to explain it away is to blame it all on a small group of evil men – the Nazis. No one else in Germany admitted to knowing what was going on until it was established that they must have done but then they were 'only obeying orders'. The outside world had no idea what was taking place – really! Prominent Jews who had managed to escape were doing their best to publicise what was going on and every major player had their own intelligence services, the most far reaching one being that of the Vatican through its confessional system.

Now the term Nazi is used as a label to attack anyone or any organisation with different views to their own. It is an alternative to reasoned analysis and sensible discussion.

Genes, Upbringing or Chance?

'What has made me what I am?' is a question many people will have asked themselves at some time during their lives.

Few would disagree with the importance of upbringing. A child brought up in a household with well stocked bookshelves will see reading as something that they want to do to find out what their parents are doing. Parents reading to children or telling them bedtime stories whets their appetites even more. A child who sees their first book when they start school has no such motivation and in extreme cases they may remain illiterate for the rest of their lives.

The same principle applies to physical activity. If parents are physically active children will automatically see going for walks and playing games and sports as the 'natural' thing to do. If parents spend most of their time in front of a television screen children will see passive entertainment as 'natural'.

The element of chance or luck is something which can play a very big part in anyone's life. Many of our stars and heroes will point to a turning point in their career when they got their 'big break'. One of the most interesting examples of this is the Scottish lady, Susan Boyle, who had spent most of her life in very humble circumstances singing at local pubs and clubs for very little until she appeared on a television program.

For others their 'big break' may not have been appreciated or understood at the time. For me it was passing the exam which enabled me to go to a Grammar School. It was a very close call. I took it for the first time when I was below the 'average age' and suffering from one of my many childhood illnesses and I failed it. Few people at that time got a second chance; I was very lucky to have one. My brother only got the one chance and failed and from then on his opportunities in life were more limited than mine were.

Upbringing and chance are not controversial topics in principle although details may be. So what about the one that is highly controversial – genes?

No one would now argue that two parents who have hair with a distinctive colour such as red are likely to produce children with the same feature. Neither would they expect two dwarfs to produce a very tall child. There are many genetic features which we take for granted. Some women will take this much further than I would. When seeing a young baby for the first time I have often heard "doesn't he look like his father," or "doesn't she look like her mother," depending on the sex. I am a bit of a cynic on this one unless there is a clear distinguishing feature such as the dimple Michel Douglas inherited from his farther Kirk. Of course I admit to the possibility that their powers of observation in such matters are more finely tuned than mine are.

So what about intelligence; why should that be any different from other inherited features? The simple answer is that it is not and I have never seen any published work to contradict this. One of the latest pieces of research to confirm it was led by Professor Ian Deary at the University of Edinburgh and the results of the work he supervised was published in the October 2011 issue of the journal of Molecular Psychiatry.

The study involved 3,511 unrelated adults which is quite an impressive number for this type of work. The report concluded that 40% of the variation in knowledge and 51% of the variation in problem solving skills could be accounted for by the differences in the DNA of the individuals involved.

It is interesting that the general media seems to have ignored this work; I only found one exception – by Alok Jha, the Guardian science correspondent – when I did my own research.

There is still time of course and something might be in the pipeline as I am writing this; however I doubt it, any serious discussion would be bound to lead to some of society's taboos and everyone involved would soon be categorised as Nazis.

I don't have any job or reputation to worry about so I have no problem in using all the evidence I can find to challenge some of society's taboos and, more importantly, to offer some solutions.

A Licence to have Children?

We live in a society where licences are required to take part in many different activities. Some examples that most people will be familiar with are as follows:

1. **Drive a vehicle on public roads**. To obtain a licence to drive on public roads now requires both a practical and a written test. For most of us this only involves a licence to drive a car. For others far more stringent tests are required. For example the PSV licence to drive a bus and the most difficult of all; the Heavy Goods licence to drive an articulated lorry. This was not always the case; my father had a UK licence without passing any test and I can remember driving on the continent in the late nineteen sixties when no test or licence was required. Nowadays very few people would try and make out a case for not having a test although there will always be controversy as to whether the tests are too stringent or not tough enough.

2. **Keep a public house**. There is a sign above the main entrance of every pub in the land which gives the name of the licensee. He has to satisfy the local magistrate that he is a fit and proper person to undertake such work. Since most of our pubs are owned by large companies he will also have had to go through a comprehensive training scheme.

3. **Keep a shotgun or rifle**. There are separate licences required for each type of firearm and stringent rules about where they are stored in secure cabinets and how they may be transported from one place to another. There are two reasons for members of the public to keep deadly weapons. One is control of wildlife and the other is for sport. Foxes are shot when they are threatening poultry. Grouse and pheasants are shot purely for sport. Deer are shot for both sport and when they are causing damage to either crops or trees.

4. **Keep a bird of prey**. The licences for owning or breeding birds of prey are very stringent. I have been fortunate enough to have

spent some time with some of the people involved with hawks, owls and falcons and I have a picture of me with a Harris hawk on my arm behind me as I am writing this. Birds of prey are trained either for hunting or simply for demonstration purposes. Whenever a bird of prey is let free it is fitted with a tracking device. For the Harris hawk there is a very practical reason for this. It has become one of the most popular birds for falconers to keep because they are not only easier to train than many other species but they are also prolific breeders and therefore relatively cheap. They are one of the few birds of prey which often hunt in groups in the wild. Their natural habitat is the USA which makes them an alien species. If all attempts to retrieve a Harris hawk fail it must be reported at once and it is shot.

The list is by no means exhaustive and I have no doubt that the reader can think of many other examples of where a licence is sensibly required.

In the author's opinion one of the **most responsible and challenging undertakings for anyone is to bring another human being into this world,** and yet no training or licence is required. All it needs is a moment of irresponsible sex and the process has already started.

A test for the suitability of a couple to start a family could include the following:

(1)   A genetic check up.

(2)   Suitable accommodation

(3)   Economic check up

(4)   A parenting course

Let us look at each one of these in some detail:

Genetic Check

For many years some people have been aware of a genetic 'fault' in their family. Among their ancestral history there have been individuals who have suffered a crippling mental or physical disability. These often result in a very limited life span for the child.

Since the genetic code was cracked by James Watson and Francis Crick the advances in understanding human DNA have been incredible; there is even a self test kit for some conditions now available on the net.

For very little cost two prospective parents can have their DNA checked and matched to accurately assess the probability of any offspring they produce having a serious genetic problem.

For the vast majority of people the result of this test would be a simple OK – no serious problems are predicted. For a small minority the test would reveal a high or very high chance of a genetic deformity. The reader may well ask what I mean by the terms 'high' and 'very high'. Unlike a politician I will not dodge the issue and tentatively suggest that any figure above a one in four chance is very high and above one in ten is high.

Whatever the figure, the couple would need a preliminary counselling session when they would be made aware of all the implications and then given some time out to think about it before a second meeting.

At the end of the second counselling session the couple may have decided that they have gone off the idea of having a child and withdraw their application for a licence. There is of course now another possible option for people without dogmatic religious views – selective abortion. At an early stage in the pregnancy a sample of the foetus DNA could be checked for the faulty gene. In the majority of cases this would produce a positive result and the parents could look forward to having a healthy child. However there would always be some cases when they would have the heartbreak of deciding whether they would want to try again.

I remember reading in the press about a couple whose first two children had Downs syndrome. Consequently, their DNA had been checked and matched. The result predicted that any further child they might have would have a very, very high chance of having that genetic fault. They had decided to try once more to produce a healthy child. They were hailed as courageous heroes by the press for being so brave. My reaction was one of sadness and depression that people should behave in such an irresponsible way and that they were treated by our headline-seeking media the way they were. For every couple behaving like that there must be hundreds or even thousands who have taken a more responsible course of action but they never make the news.

A considered and responsible application of genetics could see many crippling ailments reduced to the history books in a few generations in the same way that immunisation has for many diseases.

Accommodation

This would be quite straightforward compared with the previous test. The applicants would simply have to provide evidence that they already had, or would have by the time a child was born, accommodation which was suitable.

Two bedroom home for a first child and a three bedroom home for a second would quickly 'tick the box'. It could include shared accommodation in some cases where, for example, grandparents had a large house. A case which springs to mind is a farm where two generations would be working from and living in the same home. However this would require everyone involved to be interviewed to make sure that each of them understood what they would be taking on and was aware of the potential pitfalls.

One of the most important and contentious issues this check is designed to stop is 'child first', jump the queue for social housing and 'accommodation later'. This is not only unfair to responsible people in the queue; it is a clear sign that any child would not be brought up in a suitable environment.

Economic Check

This check would have a similar format to applying for a mortgage on a house. The prospective parents would simply have to demonstrate that they were in a stable relationship and had sufficient funds and reliable income to provide for a child without relying on state benefits other than automatic ones such as a child allowance.

Parenting Course

This is a relatively new development which I only know about from what I have read and heard about from people of my children's generation. No-one of my generation went on one but I soon learned how to fold nappies differently for boys and girls. (Easy for an engineer to remember – any fluid that starts going up will carry on in that direction until absorbed and vice versa.) I probably took more interest than many men of my generation in the early development of my children despite having so many other distractions.

My daughter's first visit to the swimming pool was before she could walk and I soon found that we could go on more adventurous walks without the clutter of a pram by letting her spend most of the time on my shoulders in between inspecting items of interest. I also discovered that the cheapest peanuts, the ones that nowadays people only ever feed to the birds, were a very nourishing supplement to expensive baby foods. Of course they had to be well chewed before she could digest them and she would often eat them faster than I could chew them.

The new parenting courses are an excellent idea which every prospective parent should take, not only for a first child but for a second so that they are aware of the impact of a new baby on a sibling. Anyone declining to take one would need to provide a very good reason why they should be exempt.

Single parents

The above tests for a licence have been worded in the plural on the assumption that two parents are involved which I believe is the ideal. However I would not rule out applications from a single mother but she would still have to pass the same basic tests.

Licence Granted

For responsible young people the above checks would be simply formalising the issues which they would have considered anyway, although a check list is always handy to make sure nothing has been omitted.

Once they had been granted a licence to have a child they should be given maximum support by the state. To keep the Income Tax system as simple as possible, there would be no change to any tax code. The extra support would take the form of a fixed benefit which should be higher than the present one for the first child and provision of free nursery care and other ongoing help.

For a second child the benefit should be significantly reduced to say half the benefit for the first child. The ongoing help would of course continue.

For a third and subsequent child there should be no benefit - only the ongoing help.

For some of society's most successful couples these rules would not be a deterrent to having a large family; there would be very few people in this position.

The reason for tapering off the benefits system is to fit in with a planned population policy. Our country is already overcrowded and if we cannot take measures to put our own house in order we are not in a position to criticise other countries with more severe problems. Successful people are already having smaller families and a licensing system would have little effect on them.

Application Failed

There is no point in having any licensing system if it can be simply ignored. If no licence is granted there could be an appeal against the decision but if the decision is upheld the only concern should be for the welfare of the child.

No child should start off their life in an unsatisfactory environment and they should be protected from that fate. The only way to do this is for the state to take over and place the child in a more satisfactory environment.

Adoption

The first alternative is clearly adoption. There are always couples who are unable to have a child and would have no problems in passing any test to bring up a child. I know one such couple very well. The child they adopted is now grown up with her own family. At an appropriate stage she was told of her situation but she has never worried about her origins; she is just grateful for having two loving parents who mean so much to her. She went to university and now has a very successful career.

There are currently some very strange attitudes to adoption in the UK which has led to fewer and fewer children being adopted. The rules and regulations applied by the politically correct gang are so arduous that they hardly ever seem to be able to match a child with prospective parents. If the prospective parents have passed the test to bring up a child, that is all that should be required. The prospective parents should of course be given full details of the child's background so that they are fully aware of what they are taking on.

If any pregnancy is in an early stage abortion is another alternative which should be encouraged. This applies particularly to school children who may grow up to one day pass the test with flying colours and have their child when their time is right.

Fostering

This may be regarded as short term adoption and as such will seldom be as satisfactory as full adoption. One situation where it might be the ideal solution is where the biological parents are not in a position to bring up a child but are likely to be at some time in the future. It might also be the correct decision where the father of the child is unknown.

Orphanages

Orphanages have historically been given a bad name as 'institutions' associated with exploitation and abuse; care must be taken not to repeat these mistakes.

Orphanages should be run by the state and suitable staff carefully vetted and monitored. With so many people now taking courses to qualify them to become carers it should not be too difficult to find staff.

Boarding Schools

Some of the best schools in the land have boarding pupils. At one extreme everyone may be boarding; at the other extreme 20% is about the minimum to make this provision worthwhile. Boarding schools are normally 'public' i.e. private fee paying but this is not always the case; I was a day boy at a state Grammar School with one of the school 'houses' consisting of all the boarding pupils.

Although some of the young people starting out in life at an orphanage might spend all their formative years there, this is not ideal. The brightest ones should be integrated into the existing boarding school system at the earliest possible age.

For the majority, a new type of boarding school should be developed for pupils with limited academic ability. Their expectations should not be built up to believe they can 'be anything they want to be'. They must however be brought up to believe that they can make a worthwhile contribution to society by training for a job within their capabilities.

Boarding schools might seem an expensive option for the taxpayer but I am confident it would work out cheaper than some of the present day alternatives which seem to be producing people who feel alienated from society. They would also eliminate the 'ping pong blame game' often played by so many of our present leaders. Integrating 'home life' with school life would eliminate this completely.

The underclass

The introduction to this chapter was the rioting in the summer of 2011 where the term 'underclass' became widely used. Four months later there have been many attempts to analyses the composition of the underclass. A common theme is that the majority are receiving benefits of some kind. In the most extreme cases there are families where no one has worked for three generations. Almost all were living in public funded housing of one form or other. There were many single parent families and the older the matriarch of a household became the larger became the size of the family. Then there were drugs; there were very few cases where no one in a family was involved in some way. It is not too surprising that over 50% of those identified as being involved in the riots were already known to the police.

Gang membership was another common factor but reliable figures for membership of illegal organisations are impossible.

During the same period of time our 'leaders' have been offering a variety of solutions most of which seem to be throwing money at the problem. One of the simplest and craziest proposals is to increase state benefits for 'problem families'. With no control over how the money is spent it is just as likely to be spent on drugs as anything else.

A more sensible and thought out solution is to provide more sport and leisure facilities to "keep the kids of the streets". Few people would argue against this one but it should not only apply to 'problem children' but to all our young people. Adventure holidays both in the UK and at more exotic locations abroad are also proposed to broaden the horizons of the criminal youth. Talks in schools by ex gang members and drug users as well as by successful sporting personalities might all make a worthwhile contribution to the problem and should be encouraged.

A number of reports have emerged which centre on the behaviour of the police. Some of these seem to go from one extreme to the other, with heavy handed behaviour by the police before the riots being offered as one of the main causes of the riots. During the riots they were accused of just standing by and watching instead of taking firm action. At the time of writing it is being proposed that the police should be armed and should be able to use their discretion on when to use their weapons. The lawyers must be already rubbing their hands at the thought of all the work this could provide them with.

Conclusions

Any reader will no doubt have formed some of their own opinions and thought of some potential solutions to the riots before reading this chapter. Now all I ask is for them to reflect on their own deliberations and those of our leaders to decide how confident they are that "it could never happen again."

The solutions other people have been offering can be categorised as medium term at the best and quick fix at the worst. None of them tackle the long term problems and never will as long as the present eugenic policies of our governments continue to promote growth in the underclass relative to the rest of the population.

My ideas may be radical and taboo but perhaps not so audacious as those of Copernicus when he upset the churches of the day by suggesting that the earth was not at the centre of the universe.

EDUCATION

My first primary school was a very small one which probably had no more than a hundred pupils. It was in a small village about a mile away from where I lived. There were no roads to cross and most of the way followed a path across open fields. After being taken there a couple of times by one of my parents I used to make my own way there and back. I am not sure exactly how long I spent at that school.

My next school was a secondary school where most pupils stayed until the age of 15 which was then the school leaving age. This was about three miles away but there was public transport and I had a free bus pass. Unfortunately two buses were involved each covering about half the trip and if I missed a connection it was quicker to walk the last bit. In summer I would often walk all the way back, taking a short cut down a small lane and along the canal tow path.

Discipline at the school was very strict and one of my friends was once so badly beaten that his father went to the school. That was the only time I can recall that happening; normally we were only hit when we deserved it and our parents would have approved and just told us to watch our behaviour in class.

If I could remember their names I would like to be able to thank many of my teachers from Hutton Grammar School although I expect they will all now be dead. The school was over 400 years old with a large boarding contingency. The Latin motto translated to "work or leave". Discipline was something the modern generation will find hard to believe. Each teacher had his own instrument of punishment; a cane, a belt or a slipper and even the prefects could join in. Just before I left one prefect saw me not wearing my battered school cap on the way to school. He had his moment of sadism but was fortunate that I never saw him again after I left. I had a strange relationship with that school. At 16 I had captained the school water polo team, played at board two in the chess team and always did quite well academically, particularly in the science subjects, and yet I never quite fitted in and my expulsion was discussed more than once. On reflection my problems originated from my class background. In my year there were only two other pupils whose parents could be described as working class and we all left without even considering entering the sixth form. I did not appreciate it at the time but that school gave me a solid foundation for my future career.

Overview of the UK

In 2007, a UNICEF, (the United Nations organisation for children's rights) report put the issue of child well-being firmly on the UK's political agenda. When compared with 20 other advanced countries, including substantially poorer ones such as Greece and Poland, the UK did not fare very well. It was third from bottom for educational standards, bottom for self-esteem, and second from bottom for teenage pregnancies resulting in an overall bottom of a table for child welfare

As a result of the UNICEF report the British branch commissioned a more limited survey to compare children's experiences in the UK with those of children in Spain and Sweden. Dr Agnes Nairn was author of the report published in 2011 which used Ipsos MORI to collect statistics and was paid for by the Department for Education. Once again the UK came out very badly. The key conclusions in the report were: "What we found has serious implications for how we move forward as a society and how we tackle the impact that materialism and inequality have on children's well-being" and "The main reason for UK children performing so badly was attributed to a 'materialistic culture' and children spending insufficient time with their parents."

The present situation in the UK.

We will start at primary or pre-school education. There are those who come from families who are familiar with books. They will have been brought up with a well stocked library and they have watched their parents read all their lives. What their parents do is what they want to do also. They are the ones whose parents read a bedtime story every night and soon they will want to do the same. They are the ones who will have learned their alphabet and read a few simple books before they ever come to school.

At the other end of the spectrum there are those will never have seen a book before. They may have seen a games console ' to keep them quiet', but nothing will interfere with the evening's television for the adult members of the family. Eventually they go up to bed without a bedtime story. One advantage these children have is to be more 'street wise' because they are more likely to be allowed out, unsupervised during the day.

The first few days at school are a very traumatic experience for both the staff and students. Some with friends will already know some of the fellow pupils; others may not. It is time for making new friends and mixing. The first few days will be spent on 'games' but it will be a very short time before the serious business of learning how to become a useful citizen in today's world. It is the time when the student to staff ratio is at a maximum.

One of the basics a child must be aware of is just how far they can go in terms of contributing and disrupting a class. This can be a very fine line between the two and most good teachers will recognise this.

There are those pupils will put up a hand to answer any question but those who will not - even when they know the answer. Then there will be one or two who will be totally disruptive when they are asked to do anything. This should first of all be raised with the parents who can see it is as much in their interest as it is in the schools and hopefully put an end to it. However there will be some who are quite prepared to leave discipline to the school – 'we can't control him either'.

I firmly belief that discipline should start right at the beginning as soon as a child is disruptive in class. A child who is repeatedly disruptive can be taken to the head teacher and given corporal punishment, with some other designated member of staff to act as a witness to what is taking place. All that is needed is ruler to the hands or buttocks - no 'clip around the ears' or anything which could cause permanent damage.

My granddaughter was exposed to disruption in her first school. The whole class were in agreement with her but the lad was also a bully and got away with it for far too long. Eventually the school decided that he should have a class of his own. One to one tuition – hardly an ideal use of resources. If he had been given a measure of corporal punishment this might never had got to that stage. Incidentally my granddaughters went to a rural school and in all other respects it was excellent. I shudder to think about some of the inner city schools.

High School/Grammar/Public Schools.

I have always been against Public schools – a misnomer if ever there was one. I believe that education in earned by merit alone and not the ability to pay. However I also believe that one should get the best education that is available, quite a conundrum.

My daughter attended the local high school up to about the age of thirteen. My marriage was over by then but I still visited the kids every day. I was visiting her one day when I enquired about home-work. She said she never had any. I knew that I was at a Grammar School when I was thirteen and I never had a day without any. I had already realised that she lacked ambition. She was thinking of being a hairdresser or working in a local shop. This is the girl who I once taught the fundamentals of reading before primary school. Subsequently I found that they were being taught the ITA (Initial Teaching Alphabet). I remember getting myself up to speed until I knew how to help her with the bedtime stories and ITA. I soon started to write my first bedtime stories in ITA – the school had a very limited library.

Now all ambition had gone and it was a worry to me. Then my ex-wife's husband came up with a solution – they should send her to a private school. It was like a red rag to a bull – I was dead against it. My opposition did not last long as soon as I saw the results. Within a few short months she got homework every night and her outlook on life completely changed. Peer pressure can do wonderful things. Eventually she was in a background when everyone seemed to be working to achieve the maximum and not the minimum. It was now a matter of 'what subjects will I be studying at university'.

My two sons followed later to another public school (they were all in single sex schools). I reluctantly offered to contribute half but without my present wife's contribution I could never have managed it with a Lecturers salary. All three went on to higher education. My daughter went on to study for a degree in dentistry. I often wonder how they might have got on at the local high school.

Discipline

It always goes back to the question of discipline which should have been taught from the first day in primary school. My sons where subject to harsh treatment at their public schools just I had been at a grammar school. Some times over the top with their beatings, but I never remember any complaints until well after when we reminisce.

The new generation has been influenced by the 'you can not touch me or you will be in trouble'. Fortunately my granddaughters are now at a grammar school were there does not seem to be any discipline issues. They of course have detentions and the ultimate weapon they have is expulsion.

A few years ago when the new 'discipline' had started to take hold I met an ex colleague of mine. I asked about his wife who was also a teacher. He replied that she could not wait until the day she could retire. He gave me one example which shocked me and I am not easily shocked. A fifteen year old had been caught bullying and she simply asked him "how would you like it if it had been done to you". He replied "how would you like it if I suggested a fuck ". She never did anything about it; she had seen it all before and could not wait to get out.

Many of our new teachers feel the same and stress related illnesses are something I now understand. So much for the new way of 'discipline', I think we should have a rethink on what we have now and it should start from the very beginning at primary school.

Higher Education

Higher education should be free and available to all who can benefit from it. No tuition fees and the grant which goes with it are automatically taken care off by my chapter on economics.

We have come a long way since I was at university when about 5% of the population could benefit from it. There is no doubt that this should be higher but for the idealist who thinks it should be 100% it is pie in the sky. We have already gone over the top on higher education.

We now have a shortage of skilled artisans and tradesmen. When I was at university it would have been laughable if someone then suggested that a plumber could earn more than a teacher. At each stage in a society's development there will be requirements for people to fulfil various roles. Before the industrial revolution we were an agricultural society and most people were employed there. Now we must keep up with the times and ask ourselves what we now require.

It is no good training people where there is no job to offer them. It simply builds up expectations when they realise that there is no work. A growth industry has been build along the lines of 'bums on seats' and what ever the student wants they should get. Inevitably this has lowered standards to the lowest common denominator.

Statistics

UK Total 2011/12	2,496,645
Undergraduates	1,928,140
Post Graduates	568,505
Staff	378,250
Academic	181,385
Non-academic	196,860
Undergraduates to Academic staff/student ratios	10.6

Many of the people now classed at post graduates are top-up students who want to, say, take an MBA to top up a BSc in economics. There are still a surprising number of students who wish to study for a

PhD, but I understand that this is composed of a lot of foreign students. It is interesting that the 196,860 non-academic staff now outnumber the academic staff. There are secretaries and technicians who will account for some of this, but there will be administrators who will be obsessed with 'the bums on seats' syndrome irrespective of the social implications. We need more engineers but they are not very staff/student friendly.

Increasingly the more graduates we produce the more likely they are to be dissatisfied with their outcome. Some are still without jobs when the new graduates appear to compete with them. Either that or they have finally accepted that they must expect jobs with a below graduate entry requirement.

The debts

The growth in higher education has slowed down this year because of the iniquitous debts caused by student loans and fees. From now on students will face an average debt of £30,000 when they graduate. Provided that they are taking the right courses, everyone benefits whether they have children or not – who will pay for the time when they can no longer work? They should come out of university free of debt. They can pay later by taxation when they are better able to do this – by the time when they have produced the next generation.

Now the latest graduates spend their time paying off their debts before they start to have children. They will then have typically one or two. At the other end of the spectrum we have produced a generation of underclass where there are several generations without a job and they are producing children in a 'benefit culture'. They know that the more children they have the better will be their standard of living. I have covered this in detail in my chapter on eugenics.

Foreign Students.

Where we have reciprocal agreements they should not be made to pay either. Otherwise they should pay.

Continuous Assessments

This has crept into high schools and higher education alike and it has gone over the top. Many years ago when it first came in, I had a friend who taught at one educational establishment and his son was at a different establishment. His advice was to just concentrate on exams and he would take care of the project. I tried to point out that a little helping hand is acceptable but that was too much. He had already developed a cynicism of continuous assessment and he would have none of it. His son went on to study in higher education and was successful in graduating with a BSc.

Now a very high proportion of educational establishments use continuous assessments to monitor student's progress. I can see the point of using, and becoming familiar with the Internet – I do it all the time to check my facts. But now it has got to the stage where you can purchase whole essays, and even project work for degrees, online.. Any student with common sense will modify these to suit their own style and I pity the supervisor who can discern the difference between the student's own work and plagiarism. It has now become an issue of how much you are prepared to pay to get a first class essay.

What has happened to the good old exams when you were sat down for three hours, without any assistance, to see what you had learned from the course? One argument against this is that some people get nervous and are incapable of producing their best work in an exam condition. I suspect this applies to a very small minority. It also reflects life in general. There are many points where you will 'be put on the spot'; interviews, presentations, and just boring old routine things where you just made an honest mistake. (Only last week I met an otherwise very sensible householder who could not recall where the stop tap was located during a plumbing emergency.)

About turn

One of the latest 'government initiatives' is to encourage young people to go straight from school into apprenticeships, thus avoiding the dreaded student debts. Some of these include much needed engineering apprenticeships where the majority will stay as skilled engineers for the rest of their lives.

However the government does not stop there. It offers a route to the professions. Banking, accountancy, law and the means to become professional engineers are all included. This new initiative is something which was always the case when I was first a student. Many years later when I was a staff member I recall being one of the last ones to take a class leading to professional engineering status. It was a tough course, demanding on the staff as well as the students – the pass rate was very low. I suspect that the pass rate will remain low unless there is a dip in standards again.

Students

There is seldom a week goes by without another of those 'innovations' which seems to be successful tried in one school and others should take the same direction. Within a single school these does not take into account the enthusiasm of the staff involved. Some enthusiastic staff could make anything work; change the staff and it won't work as well. What we do not want is staff who 'cannot wait until they retire' and they have to accept that demography has changed and that they can no longer retire at 60 or 65. Some discipline could go a long way to helping that happen.

CHARITIES

The modern rules and priorities of charities both old and new seem to be:

1. Make sure that it fronted by a big name; royalty, sports idols and TV or film stars are ideal. This gives an immediate impact and an instantaneous pool of potential donors.

2. Appoint professional organisers who know how to con and manipulate the public; political spin doctors are ideal.

3. Start a publicity campaign on all fronts from the mass media to maximising the use of caring 'foot soldiers' who will freely give up their time organising local sponsorship events such as "run a mile to help the three blind mice".

4. An effective campaign will soon be bringing in enough cash to cover the exorbitant salaries and expenses of the organisers.

5. Think about how they can spend some of the money on the needy who the charity is purporting to support and hence justify the existence of the organisation.

6. If the beneficiaries of the charity are overseas they may receive very little. The charity may have been set up to provide say twenty schools in a remote area of some African country. A local

politician will give his time 'freely' to the project knowing that there will be lots of expenses, consultant's fees, contracts for work done and work not done with backhanders which will all be tax free. It is important that he ensures that one of the schools is completed to an impressive standard.

7. The next step is to bring in the media again (all expenses paid and well looked after). Ideally now the big name celebrity should be there; sitting in on a typical class, giving a brief address or perhaps even a lesson and of course playing with the children outside the classrooms. There is no need for any subterfuge for this part of the operation. The kids involved are genuinely grateful and happy with their transformed lives and fired ambitions to do well for themselves and their country. Donors in the country where the money came from will see their contributions as being well spent and contribute more money.

8. Sufficient money may well have been raised to provide fifty schools but after all the deductions for organisers various remunerations and the backhanders for local politicians there was only ever sufficient funds left over to provide one school and the other nineteen could be conveniently forgotten. Time to move on to the next charity.

Children in need

I have already covered some of this in the Chapter on the World Population Crisis under famines. In this chapter I will concentrate on the needs in the UK.

One of the beneficiaries of the fund was a group of school children from one of the deprived areas of Birmingham. Some of the money raised had been used to provide them with a football strip and a pair of one of the most upmarket designer boots. They were shown getting coaching and encouragement from local professional players who impressed on them that if they worked hard they too could follow in their footsteps.

They all seemed to be having a lot of fun which was nice to watch and for many of them their day on the television will be the highlight of their childhood and the envy of kids who where not there.

However after all the fun and laughter has subsided just what is likely to have been achieved? The chances that any of them will fulfil their ambitions to become professional footballers are very remote and they will become disillusioned. The idea that posh designer, must have, boots are of prime importance will have been reinforced.

The most memorable part of the program was when one of the children was asked who he wanted to play for. Without hesitation he replied Manchester United; not one of the local teams, Birmingham, Aston Villa or even West Bromwich Albion.

They had clearly been raised with commercial television and the press telling people that only four or five teams in the Premier Division had a chance of doing well – sadly that is true.

If just one of the children did make it to becoming a professional footballer – very unlikely. The rest they would face the prospect of getting a job or no job at all. It made good television but their expectations were unrealistic.

At the same time the government continues to close playing fields in schools and elsewhere which can benefit all children.

I take my hat off to those professional footballers who genuinely give up their own time and money to help sport. All too often it is a 'celebrity' who will make an appearance until the cameras have gone and it is just another chore to the sponsors who continue to support 'celebrities'.

Charities that should not rely on charity donations.

There are several charities that come into this category but I will just give an example to show what I mean:

The Lifeboat men/women have a long history of coming to the aid of mariners who have run into difficulties at sea. They used to be powered by oars on a slipway close to the sea in their port. They were all locals who were familiar with the use of oars and required minimum training.

The technological revolution has come to help the Lifeboat men/women. There are now 'All-weather' boats with a range of 150-250 nautical miles. They can withstand very heavy weather conditions far away from base. They train in daylight, fog and darkness and remain at the scene for hours helping to pick up any survivors.

It is not economic to have an 'All-weather' boat in every port and a smaller inshore rescue boat will still be serving some ports. These are sufficient for many incidents or perhaps serve until an 'All-weather' boat arrives. They no longer rely on oars for propulsion.

All this requires training to a very high standard and the list of what is required can be found on the web. Sometimes their training will involve being away from home. They need special kit particularly if there is any need to go overboard to facilitate a rescue.

They are still volunteers who give up their time to rescue mariners. I do not think that that they should have the extra burden of being away from home or raising money for kit.

Any sea going boat or ship which is capable of going past the harbour bar must have insurance. The reader will recall some marinas where there are a plethora of boats which sometimes are only used a couple of times a year. They should all be insured. At the moment this is a handy tax revenue for the exchequer. The money raised would be more than enough to finance the entire Lifeboat's needs and what is left over the exchequer can have.

Sponsorship

A few years ago I noticed a sponsored swim in Lake Windermere and I decided to investigate further. I got the details and I decided it could be an excuse for a family reunion and when we had finished it would of course be a traditional family reunion with plenty of beer.

I circulated the family and they were all for it. I intended it to be a grandfather, a son in law and my youngest grandson taking part. The latter, Connor, would have to lie a bit since he was only ten at the time but he was by far the better swimmer and there was no doubt about him. My son in law, Dave, was already into triathlons and I was regularly swimming a mile at the baths but I knew I would need to step up my training closer to the date.

There was an upfront payment to reserve a place, which I did. My two sons would also be there but although they are competent swimmers they had never managed a mile and would be looking after the beer!

One by one they dropped out until it was left to just me alone and there was no way I was going up Windermere on my own. I informed to sponsors so that others could take our reserved places. In 2012 Connor had to lie about his age once more, he was sixteen at the time. He wanted to take part in the Poole harbour swim which was 4.8 miles around Brownsea Island and despite not having a wet suit he came second!

Ever since 2006 I get reminders about the Windermere swim and how I can drum up a sponsorship list to get others to pay for it. I did not need anyone's help then and I do not now.

Perhaps I am being a little bit hard on sponsorships; I know some of those and everything goes to the charity they are supporting. There are others where the sponsorship goes into the expenditure incurred, and very little is left for the charitable causes.

I now only support the family when it comes down to sponsorship; they provide their own expenses and the proceeds will go directly to a local charity.

RELIGION

My own religious upbringing would best be described as Church of England. I was a product of a mother who had been brought up as a Catholic and a father who had been brought up in the Church of England. My mother's family had its own division. My grandfather was a protestant and my grandmother a Catholic but all their children went to Catholic schools. The confusion on the maternal side of the family resulted in my uncle Bob supporting Liverpool and my uncle Ted supporting Everton. My paternal grandparents were more united and shortly after I was born they insisted that I was christened in the Church of England.

The Church of England variant of the Christian faith was taught at all the schools I attended. I was being indoctrinated but it was a relatively mild form of indoctrination compared with what many people I met later in life underwent. I learned the 'Lord's Prayer' and the words to some of the more stirring hymns. Some of the latter are very good of course and even now I am quite happy to join in singing them – particularly the ones associated with sporting events.

I can vaguely remember being taught to pray before I went to sleep; just as I can remember that I probably believed in Santa Claus in my very early days. The only difference is that I remember Santa delivered on time but I can never remember God doing very much in response to my humble requests. Before I reached my teens I found that masturbating was a more satisfying way to end the day although of course I felt guilty about it – sex was a taboo subject in my family.

Before I went to Grammar school I never thought too deeply about religion; all my spare time was spent taking part in sports or exploring the countryside around the area where I lived. I went fishing, shooting with a catapult, collecting all sorts of things from bird's eggs to humble leaves. I also had responsibilities such as looking after my pet rabbits.

I first started to question some of the things I had been taught in RI; (which is an abbreviation for religious instruction and also for religious indoctrination), shortly after starting at Hutton Grammar School.

There was a broad curriculum and I was always one of the first to ask questions on any subject. I soon found that there was a 'logic order' in the responses I got to my questions. Any questions I asked in Maths, Physics or Chemistry classes were answered in a clear logical way that increased my understanding of the subject.

At the bottom of my 'logic order' were English and RI. I could see no logic in some of the rules I was taught in English such as the "i before e except after c" with a plethora of exceptions to the 'rule'. However RI was far worse. I never seemed to get any satisfactory answers to my questions. I can remember replies such as 'you just have to accept' and 'you just have to have believe' because it is in the Bible. For me, lack of answers just provoked supplementary questions and I was often told to shut up because I was disrupting the class. Far from increasing my indoctrination, those RI classes sowed the seeds of enlightenment and freedom from any religious belief.

By my early teens I was reasonably well read for my age and knew something about other religions; certainly enough to realise that my specific indoctrination was just an accident of birth and if I had been born in another country or even another household in this country I might have had an early indoctrination in a different religion.

I found religion to be a fascinating subject and with no answers from school I discussed it with friends and adults whenever I got the opportunity.

Neither my mother nor my father had been regular churchgoers since they had left home. After we had both had a few drinks one night I brought the subject of religion up with my father by asking the simple question "do you believe there is a god?" He thought for a while before replying; "yes, there must be". I asked for practical evidence which I could check to back up his statement. All he could come up with were the thumb and forefinger markings on a haddock where Christ had picked one up and an equally strange comment about markings on donkeys. (The haddock is a sea fish found in northern waters and the only reference I can find to a fish with the markings he described is the John Dory which is sometimes referred to as St Peter's fish and like many other strange markings in nature can be interpreted in a variety of ways.) My father was a very intelligent man and quite knowledgeable despite his lack of formal education. I am still amazed at his flimsy justification for a fundamental belief. I cannot remember ever discussing religion with my mother.

I do remember well discussing it with a middle aged lady when I lived and worked in a working man's club. She must have been collecting for a religious charity or selling magazines and as soon as she was free I had no hesitation in approaching her with some of my usual questions. At first, she listened intently to what I had to say and seemed grateful that someone was showing an interest in what she was doing – most people simply made a contribution or said "no thank you". Slowly her expression changed to one of horror as she listened to a fifteen year old questioning her fundamental beliefs. She had no answers of course and could only implore me to believe, ending by saying that she would pray for me.

I have met many such people since then and even now my barber, who is considering joining the Catholic clerical system, says he still prays for me after religion has been the 'topic of the day' during my occasional hair cuts. With older people, like my late mothers-in-law, I would never bring the subject up but I always do with anyone who I think might benefit from 'enlightenment'. The 'foot soldiers' of most religions are usually well meaning, pleasant people to know, who contribute to communities in many ways that are admirable. Their leaders and organisers are the ones who can so easily lead them into intolerance, bigotry and worse and are the dangers to any society.

The Old Testament

The Old Testament is accepted as an 'accurate' historic document not only by some Christians but also by many Jews and Muslims.

One of the 'stories' I gave a lot of thought to from an early age is about the series of plagues which led to the Israelites leaving Egypt. The plagues were intended to demonstrate the power of the God of Israel over the power of the numerous Egyptian gods which prevailed at that time. I now realise that many of these can be explained by exaggerating natural phenomena which might well have occurred; a good example of which is the plague of locusts.

The one event which cannot be explained away by anything natural is the death of the first born of all Egyptians. I have developed the following line of discussion which I use with anyone who accepts the Old Testament:

The death of the first born in Egypt.

What do you think when you read about an 'election' which results in a 99% vote of support for the leader of a country or an idea? (There is all too frequently an example to quote which had just taken place.)

It might of course happen in a very small community or one with a very limited electoral roll. The Falkland Islands, Gibraltar and some of the artificial Arab states are examples. However it is not difficult to get any reasonable thinking person to agree that an election producing such a result would be nothing other than a fraudulent, rigged election if it took place in a major country where every household was involved.

I have never met anyone who did not soon agree that there are a wide range of opinions on any serious topic and, if everyone thought the same, innovation and human progress would soon come to a standstill. Only then do I introduce the topic of the plagues of ancient Egypt.

One version of the Old Testament makes a very clear statement on the last of the plagues in Exodus; "On that same night I will pass through Egypt and strike down every firstborn – both men and animals – and I will bring judgement on all the gods of Egypt. **I am the**

LORD." Other versions have a similar statement which might be more subject to interpretation.

If God knows and understands everything he must have been aware that not all Egyptians supported their Pharaoh and although they may have kept quiet about it some must have even been sympathetic to the Israeli cause. However they all had to die - the 'guilty' and the innocent together. In some households the firstborn would have been a child and what can be more innocent than a child?

This selective genocide would have been on a scale comparable with the holocaust or the slaughter in Ruanda.

Then there are the animals; I am not a vegetarian so I must accept killing animals to provide meat. However just killing them to demonstrate 'power' reminds me of some of the cases I read about where mindless thugs torture and kill animals 'for a bit of fun'.

I can not see how any believer can reconcile those events and maintain a delusion of a 'compassionate and caring god.'

One line of discussion which I have never heard anyone else using I call the 'Christian child conundrum'. I use it with Christians whose views have changed very little over the passage of time such as the Jehovah Witnesses who I always welcome in whenever they call. I listen to what they have to say, although I have heard most of it before, before I start asking them a series of questions. They always readily agree with my questions until it comes to the point where I point out where the 'logic' is leading to.

The Christian child conundrum

A child is born innocent and free from sin and by the time it has been baptised it is part of your holy church. There is no way that it can have committed anything which could be regarded as a sin in the short interval between birth and baptism. If that child has an unfortunate accident the next day it must surely go to heaven?

If the child grows up into an adult it will commit many minor sins and possibly some not so minor. In extreme cases it may grow up become a heathen and an unrepentant mass murderer in which case it would surely not go to heaven?

Logically then, to ensure that the child finishes up in heaven a loving parent should kill the child ASAP after its baptism?

But such an abominable act would damn the parent and ensure that their own Soul never went to heaven?

This is not necessarily true if they truly repented; but even if they had denied themselves the chance to go to heaven, what greater sacrifice could one make than sacrificing their own chance to make sure that their offspring was guaranteed a place in heaven?

Recommended Reading

I can recommend the following two books to any reader who would like to pursue the intellectual matter of religion.

Richard Dawkins – The God Delusion

A C Grayling – Against all Gods.

The former has over 460 pages. It is very readable and I can not think of anything he has omitted.

In my introduction I have left everything personal. It is just how I came to my conclusions and enlightenment long before I could have the benefit of "The God Delusion" which was published in 2006.

Religion

Religion has been with us ever since the days where we were just hunters and gatherers and possibly before then. It only needed one man in the beginning to notice that life and death could be turned into advantage by being able to predict them. With it came power which could not be won on the battlefield.

They would have already built up a reputation of medical skills and poisons in preparation for this moment.

Today we can look back and see the traditions of "a happy hunting ground". The days of the week are based on old Viking traditions.

Today there are many Religions

Christianity is the most popular with over 2,200,000,000 and about half of these are Catholic. Islam is the second most popular with about 1,600,000,000 adherents. This is closely followed by Hinduism with 1,000,000,000 followers and Buddhism with about 500,000,000 adherents. Then there of 100,000,000 of Chinese religions which includes Taoism and Confucianism.

There then follows a jump down in numbers and some are fixed by locations. Shinto is associated with Japan. There are many minor religions; some are limited to India including Zoroastrianism, which was founded by the prophet Zoroaster and can claim to be one of the oldest.

Numerically insignificant is Judaism which claims to have 16,000,000 supporters worldwide. It is one of the oldest of the Abraham inspired religions and one of the most contentious.

Apart from the 'official' texts on religion there are many which analyse the roots of more that one religion; usually by non adherents. One I have some personal experience of is Buddhism. It originated in India but has spread throughout the Far East. One case is with Thailand where it is the dominant religion. It is often associated with a tolerance for a fellow man and other creatures. This is often the case but it does not stop the military pursuing a campaign of what some people would call genocide in the far South where it shares a common boarder with Malaysia.

Also, in the Far East of the country, where Thailand shares a common boarder with Laos, a small patch of the country is in dispute. Hardly anyone lives there but the bone of contention is a small shrine and several people were killed. For what – why could they not share it?

Buddhism does not stop the corruption which is rife. Some inner city 'monks' are in on it. Outside of the major cities there are Buddhists who are the friendliest people you will ever meet and are shocked by what is going on around them.

Religions that are the main threat to this planet.

The two main threats to this planet are Catholic Christianity and Islam. They are a threat not only because they refuse to limit the size of their families but they are the most intolerant of other views.

Many other religious organisations could fit into this category but they are far less significant in numbers.

The religions which are based on Abraham

Abraham predates Moses by several hundreds of years. He is the founder of the Jewish religion and was circumcised at the age of ninety nine years of age (Genesis in the New English Bible.) The Arc of the Covenant was constructed during their wandering in the lands which once stretched from modern day Egypt into Syria. It was handed down by God in Abraham's time. Eventually they reached their promised land, Israel and with it, Jerusalem which is significant in all Abraham based religions.

Whether it was climate change which brought about the Israelis' dissatisfaction with living in Jerusalem, they soon moved out. Throughout their wanderings other people had settled there and there was a need to get them out. This happened to Sodom and Gomorrah where the Israelis' God sent fire and brimstone on the unfortunate population. Perhaps he was only getting ready for Moses with the final plague killing off the firstborn of every woman and animal. Whether you believe in them or not this was time for vengeance, and quite unlike the current apologists who see God being all loving and understanding.

By the mid 1600's the last of the Abraham inspired religions was born; the rise of Islam.

Christian Religions

All three religions share the Old Testament. Christianity forms the basis of our calendar. Counting backwards anything before Jesus Christ was born is counted as B.C. (Before Christ) and counting forwards anything subsequent is classed as A.D. (The year of the Lord – Latin origin).

Most of what is written in the Bible will be well known for most UK readers. They come from the New Testament which was written by Jesus's disciples and were not put in writing until many years later. Often a few hundred years; until then they were handed down from generation to generation. There are discrepancies in their accounts.

What they do agree on is Jesus was executed and then rose from the dead three days later.

During a Jewish Feast he was taken away to the Roman hall of Justice to face Pilate the governor of Judea. The Jews accused him of claiming to be 'the king of all the Jews' and a lot more as well. He was taken to be crucified, (a normal method of punishment in those days) along side two criminals.

When he was dead, the religious leaders told Pilate about Jesus' prediction that he would rise from the dead. Pilate ordered an armed Roman guard to stay by the tomb day and night until three days had passed. On the third day some of the women followers asked if they could anoint the body prior to burial. A huge stone that had been placed over the grave had rolled back and the women entered the tomb. The tomb was empty apart from the wrappings. The armed guards saw nothing that would alarm them.

Subsequently Jesus appeared to his followers who had been present at the Last Supper prior to the events leading up to his crucifixion. He told them to spread his work to the far corners of planet and granted them a freedom of being able to do this with an ability to speak in many languages.

Rome converts to Christianity

For the next three hundred years the Christians continued to grow in numbers although it was not without setbacks. The infamous feeding of Christians to lions was one such example. Then in 312 Emperor Constantine was converted. Then it became the official Roman religion in 330 under the same Emperor.

Orthodox Christian Religions

At the same time as the followers of Jesus were spreading the word to the West other disciples were doing the same thing in the East. There are dozens of Orthodox Christians each established in the countries where they had the most converts. Today the reader is most likely to see Greek Orthodox or the Russian Orthodox churches but the others are still there.

There was great rivalry between the churches and attempts to try to unify them on many occasions. The Roman Catholic Church developed on autocratic lines. Everything passed through the Pope who was seen as Gods representative on earth.

The orthodox religions had a much more democratic structure. By the time of the first Crusades, some Crusaders treated fellow Christians in the same way that they did the Islamic armies.

The Reformation.

Johannes Gutenberg was the first to use movable type printing in 1439, when it became possible to run off multiple copies of the same text. It became a key role in the reformation, the age of enlightenment and the spread of learning to ordinary working men.

The Roman Catholic Church was now a long way from its roots in Rome. It could no longer manipulate armies to do its dirty work. The clergy grew rich, particularly those above the humble priest. The Catholic Church never forgot its Roman origin; everything was in Latin. Their argument was that it would be foolish and dangerous to let the congregation fully understand what was going on. They should be content with mindless repetitions of God's word handed down to the Pope.

But some men could not be silenced. The issue came to a head with the tithes which everyone had to pay to the Church. This was 10% of a yearly income to be paid to the Church. Many saw this as going straight back to the clergy in Rome without benefiting to local economy. There was also the sale of indulgences where the local priest thought he could get whatever seemed appropriate.

Martin Luther is the most famous of the dissenters when he nailed some of his ideas to the church doors in Wittenberg in Germany in 1517. He had been a former monk, a Catholic priest and a professor of theology. He originally wanted to reform the Catholic Church but was declared a heretic and an outlaw by the Church in Rome.

He saw that all Christians who had been baptised could interpret the word of God in a language that they knew well.

Thanks to the invention of the printing press his words were very quickly spread around nearby clergy and laymen. The printing press was also responsible for unifying the German language into what it is today.

The Pope could not raise an army and with it the dreaded inquisition to silence this dissenter. Soon the reformation had spread to countries in close proximity to Germany and they declared a freedom from Rome and their own interpretation of the scriptures.

Meanwhile, in Britain, Henry V111 was seeking a way out of his various marriages. His first wife was Catherine of Aragon, a powerful lady in the Catholic Church and there was no way the Pope would grant a divorce. He also saw how the Catholic monasteries had amassed a great wealth. Towards the end of his reign he set about the dissolution of the monasteries and declared himself as head of the Church in England.

There were then plenty of precedents in Northern Europe.

After Henry was gone there were disagreements with the Catholic minority and the newly established Church of England. In the reign of Elizabeth 1 she strongly supported the Church of England.

Then came the English Revolution and Cromwell finally finished off the Catholics. Not only did he pursue them in this county but he raised an army to pursue them across the Irish Sea where the population was mainly Roman Catholic. His barbaric treatment there is still with us today.

Offshoots of Christianity

From the days of Martin Luther to the days of Cromwell people were persecuted for having minority views. For a while they might have been tolerated but because they offer something different they seem as a threat to the 'established' religions. Many found that there was no option but to get out and emigrate.

A lot of emigrants found their way to the United States when it was just a colony. Today there is a strange mixture of sects and evangelical Christians. The Amish community originally came from the German speaking canton of Switzerland. They still have their own language and are reluctant to come to terms with modern society.

In 1681 King Charles 11 granted William Penn a charter for what is now Pennsylvania. Penn then guaranteed that across Europe others who were then suffering could make their way there free from religious persecution.

The Americans have also invented their own religion – Mormonism. They believe that an angel directed Joseph Smith in 1823 to a buried book written on golden plates containing the religious history of an ancient people. Smith published a translation of these plates in 1830 as the Book of Mormon. Smith sent missionaries far and wide to preach the restored gospel. Today each convert to Mormonism spends one year of their life as a missionary.

It is easy to see how the Early Christians came up with so many contradictions when they were not written down for hundreds of years later. But the book of Mormon is only a hundred and eighty three years old at the time of writing. Its secret whereabouts is only known to one representative. It purports that the world is only 10,000 years old – completely against archaeological specimens to show that it is much, much older than this.

And yet the Republican challenger to Barack Obama was former Massachusetts Governor Mitt Romney who firmly believed in this sort of crap.

Islam

This is the third and most recent religion based on Abraham. It is the second most numerous after Christianity and the fastest growing. The founder of Islam is the prophet Muhammad who was born about 570. He spent his early life and youth tending sheep and camels until he entered the service of a wealthy widow named Aisha, and in 624 he married her. She became the first of three wives and his first convert earning herself the title of "Mother of the Believers".

During his lifetime Muhammad had many visions through the archangel Gabriel who told him that there was one true god and the rest were his disciples. The name of the true god was Allah. The disciples/prophets ranged from Adam, Noah, Abraham, Moses and Jesus.

The Qur'an was thus handed down bit by bit from the archangel Gabriel. It told them how to do God's work and they would be rewarded in heaven. Muslims regard heaven as a place of joy with emphasis on the physical features of the lives to come to all believers. It also emphasises how Muslims must behave including charity, prayer, and respect for other men. One interesting 'trip' when Muhammad met Gabriel suggested that he should jump on a horse and be transported to an unknown destination. When he arrived there it was Jerusalem which then became the third sacred place after Mecca (where he was born) and Medina (his final resting place) in the Muslim world.

Everything that Muhammad said during his meetings with the angels his followers took down in writing; but for the majority who could not write it was then passed on orally. This founded the basis of the rote learning, which we still have today. The Qur'an is the word of God passed down to Muhammad who became the final prophet and the last until the judgement day.

At the same time as the Qur'an was being passed down another book, the Sunna, was written down explaining how we should live to be a better Muslim. It contains the five basic Pillars of Islam; the declaration of faith, praying five times a day facing Mecca, giving money to charity, fasting and a pilgrimage to Mecca at least once during a lifetime.

During Muhammad's lifetime there were great rivalries between Mecca, the administrative capital, and Medina, an industrial base. Muhammad was born in Mecca and when he first started to preach there he was treated with tolerance and amusement that one so young could know so much. Then he started to make converts and his harsh words against the false gods and those who worshiped them became less acceptable. The authorities decided to act against these new ideas and the prophet who was expounding them.

Muhammad was tipped off about the new developments and decided to leave with some of his disciples before they could be carried out. They made the long hard trip to Medina pursued by their attackers. Their pursuers gave up when they reached the outskirts of Medina and they might face another army.

In Medina Muhammad was welcome and continued to make converts. Soon he had converted the main factions in Medina and wanted to spread his word throughout Arabia. He knew this meant war because his only converts in Mecca were being persecuted.

At his next visit to seek inspiration from Gabriel he told him of his dilemma and that he had already been told 'not to kill'. Gabriel assured him that this did not apply to the 'infidels' who were resisting the call from Allah, the only true God. Then began the career of Mohammad the general; he led his armies in a series of wars with Mecca; and with

Allah on his side the result was never in doubt. By the time he died he had united all Arabia in Islam.

After Muhammad

After Muhammad had died he left no male heir who would have carried on his good work. His first wife, Aisha continued preaching and spreading the word of Islam and became much more political. Her father Abu Behr became the first caliph to succeed Muhammad, but he was getting old and was succeeded by Omar. There then became a battle for succession of who should succeed Muhammad as his representative on earth. The splits had come just as they had done in early Christianity.

In researching this I found it particularly difficult in giving precise dates to events and even some of the characters involved who change names repeatedly.

Islam today

Today Islam has spread from its origins in Arabia to Persia, Afghanistan, Turkey, Egypt, Indonesia, across the Northern tip of Africa and into the Iberian peninsular. The latter is the only place where it suffered a set back; elsewhere it has become the dominant religion.

Most Muslims are today classed as Sunni (about 80%) and Shia/Shiah (about 20%); however the are many offshoots from the basic religions. The main areas where the Shiah are dominant include Iran and Iraq. Syria has a very mixed grouping of religions with the Alawite Shiah representing no more than about 12% of the population but still, 'just', managing to stay in power. The rest are Arab Sunnis, Kurds, Armenians, Assyrians, Turkish Sunnis, Christians and probably quite a few non believers who are never counted in this part or the world.

One of the most important are in Saudi Arabia. They are nominally Sunni but with a strange offshoot of Wahhabi. They control the purse strings which is funding Islam throughout the world. If you have a Mosque near you it will have quite likely received a 'donation' from Saudi. They also control the literature which most Muslims read.

At the other end of the spectrum is the Kurds who are nominally classed as Muslims. Kurdish women never wear a veil or anything else except to keep out the cold. During feasts, weddings or other celebrations they dance with the men. This is a total taboo in most other Islamic societies.

In most of the Sunni world there are Shia minorities but in the 'artificial' Gulf States they are in the majority. The populations are very small but the majority are starting to demand equal rights which will mean a change in the way they are being governed at the present time.

Today the main population of Islam, numerically speaking, is in Indonesia. This is followed by India and Pakistan.

A variety of people classify themselves as Muslim; we should add what sort of Muslim are you? Just the same way we should add; what sort of Christian are you?

What sort of Muslim are you?

Although there are plenty of Muslims in the area around where I live; there is only one who I know personally. He originally came from Pakistan and I worked with him when I was doing some consultancy in 1993. He was new to heat transfer and I was given the task of training him. We soon discovered a love of cricket and were very soon in the same team. After a game of cricket we went to the nearest bar for a post-match analysis. He only ever drank non alcoholic drinks but insisted on paying his way even though our drinks were much more expensive. I once went for a social evening in his home; the only time I have ever been to a social event without alcohol being involved!

We lost touch for many years until he discovered my latest book on heat transfer and we have been corresponding by e-mail ever since. One of his most amusing experiences was going to a cricket match in India and he was the only one supporting Pakistan. He is a great guy and I cannot imagine him supporting any of the religious excesses now associated with Islam.

But some do support extremist action

Ever since Bin Laden went to fight in Afghanistan the world has not been the same. We know from past British experiences and others that Afghanistan is better left well alone. But then there is the Cold War and it was rapidly becoming under Soviet influence and the 'domino theory' applied to US thinking. It is of course totally ignorant of the way individual countries might behave and shows a lack of understanding of their customs.

The Soviets were there supporting one side and the US and Britain had to come in to redress, and ultimately tip, the balance on the other side. Without our intervention there would have been a dramatic change in the status of women. In the Soviet controlled areas they could go to school and freely mix.

Instead the US and men of our crack units taught them how to take down helicopters; a vital part of such warfare. Of course we were there as 'advisors' but if you see a helicopter gun ship coming towards you, if the Afghan misses, you are going to make sure that the second one hits. With unlimited funds and ammunition the tide turned and the Soviets withdrew.

The West had no idea of what they were leaving behind but the Soviet threat had been averted and they could leave to allow the Afghans to carry on with their 'democracy' and suppression of women. The Taliban had been the first to take up arms and soon they were running the country.

Bin Laden emerged as a martyr to the Muslim cause. He could have supported them from well out of the region of conflict but instead he went there himself. It is fundamental to understand why he went there. He was born a wealthy man in Saudi Arabia. Educated in the West and fluent in many languages, he could understand 'Western democracy' in all its variations. He could see the corruption in his home country. It was well known that the previous leader of Saudi was a man who was into a bottle of scotch a day and that some of the finest collection of wines were in Saudi, owned by his leader's extended family. Bin Laden could have joined them.

Instead he went to fight, not in his own corrupt land, but in far off Afghanistan.

Little is known about his religious conversion; but only what happened next. After his first experience in Afghanistan he emerged as a fighter to be respected and an example for the many that were to follow him.

Then came the September eleventh attacks in 2001 at the World Trade Centre in New York and the world has never been the same since. The methods of destruction were already there; a newly fuelled aircraft taking off not far away from the target. What was incredible was the organisation to make this possible. The jihadists' who were taking part knew they would die, but there were 19 of them spread among two Boeings 757 and two Boeings 767.

Some of them were very well educated and had a lot to look forward to in this world. They where all relatively young; the Ayatollahs who inspire them to do this sort of thing are old and they think their message is to inspire others. Yet inspire them they do; with the promise of an afterlife much richer than life on this planet; and they would have to settle for a few less virgins if they deviate from the plan.

Back to Afghanistan

Bin Laden was the obvious one who had the funds and could have pulled off something as dramatic as the attack on the World Trade Centre. As soon as the Soviets had been defeated the Taliban quickly took over. Bin Laden was reported to be hiding there. The second US involvement in Afghanistan was very quickly organised. This time they had a 'mandate' to involve other nations. There were very few who took them up on this offer with a token force. Except the British who always do what the US tells them to do in such situations.

Bin Laden was there but continued to evade them until recently when he was found in Pakistan close to one of their military bases living a 'normal' life. In the meantime the US had removed the Taliban from power and substituted one of their own lackeys in his place.

The current government is headed by Hamid Karzai and is the first leader of a government said to be elected by 'free elections'. Only the most naïve of observers could accept this mandate as being free and above board. In practise it is one of the most corrupt elections ever held. Money which was intended to fund the elections was appropriated by Karzai himself or his family who are in the government with him. Corruption is the order of the day in Afghanistan.

Hopefully our troops will come home soon and it will be left to the US who are also under pressure to leave Afghanistan. When they do eventually return there is no doubt that the Karzai regime will very quickly suffer for their corruption. It will not be too long for the Taliban to return.

Muslim demonstrations against the film "Innocence of Muslims"

In September 2012 Chris Stevens, the US ambassador to Libya, and three of his colleagues were killed when a mob burnt down the US consulate in Benghazi. Although the majority of the Libyans may have just been there to demonstrate, a key faction had clearly planned a military type of assault. They were armed with grenade launchers, Kalashnikov guns and petrol bombs. Local 'security forces' were either unwilling or unable to stop the mob who soon eliminated consulate security forces by killing them or forcing them to surrender. Once inside the compound the mob were free to loot and burn the buildings, killing anyone who got in their way.

Violent mob demonstrations soon followed in Tunisia and Egypt but the people taking part were not armed in the same way and although many people were injured the local security ensured that there were no mass killings. What these three countries had in common is that they had all recently been freed from oppressive dictatorships and were now 'on their individual roads' to establishing 'some form of democracy'.

Other Muslim countries soon joined in with violent demonstrations in Morocco, Bangladesh, Yemen and Sudan.

The main targets for all the demonstrations were US buildings but not unnaturally British embassies were included in some of them, since Tony Blair earned himself the tag of being an 'American poodle' over the last Iraq invasion. Our present government is doing little to dispel the notion or our subservience to the USA in military issues.

More peaceful demonstrations also took place in the capitals and major cities of Europe. I listened to reports of a demonstration in London as it was taking place. The BBC coverage included interviews with as wide a spectrum of views as they could muster. This included people taking part in the demonstrations. They were all emotionally fired up with indignation and horror at the way Mohammed had been insulted in the film. What struck me like a sledge hammer is when the **BBC reporters said that they had searched for a demonstrator who had actually seen the film and could not find one!** If the BBC could not find one in London where could they have found one?

It is very doubtful if any of the demonstrators in the Muslim countries had seen the film because so many items featured would be forbidden for them to look at. I wonder how many Muslims in the UK would admit to having seen the film which was very easy to find on u-tube.

I did of course watch the whole film – not just the abbreviated version, and was not very impressed with it. It was not easy to follow with time jumps from biblical times to today, with the life of Mohammed sandwiched in between. It was intended to be satirical, I think, but there was no humour. I did manage to glean some of the contentious issues about the life of Mohammed which may well be true but if I could not have written a better script I would stop writing.

There is no doubt that the Muslim view which the film mocks is a reasonable summary and was the intention of the film makers. There is also no doubt that very few people would have seen it without the publicity the Muslim world has given it.

It is a sad reflection on Islam that it cannot ignore or stand any criticism which does not bode very well for the West who bend over backwards to accommodate Muslim minorities whenever they can. The demonstrations will produce a backlash of hardening right wing views

Post Bin Laden

The US finally killed Bin Laden in circumstances which only those who took part in it will ever know for sure. It was of course already too late. He finally sorted out his martyrdom, but not before he inspired a whole generation to take up his cause.

The world must pay the price of increased security checks if we travel and we cannot go to any venue where there will be large crowds that could be a target without security – the recent Boston marathon in America is an example.

Now the scene has been set where fanatics do not hesitate to kill innocent bystanders along with 'intended targets'. We have far too many in this country but in Afghanistan, Pakistan and Iraqi it is an every day occurrence which hardly gets a mention in the media unless a Brit is involved.

We have also witnessed the mindless observers who support them without ever seeing the film firsthand; they only get to know by the Ayatollahs who egg them on – presumably they have seen it?

A summary of three religions.

The Jews

The Jews are the most ancient of the Abraham religions. Today they number about fourteen million with just over half of them resident in Israel but the Jews in America follow closely behind with just over five million. In the UK there are about 300,000.

Although the Jews comprise only about 0.2% of the world's population they have featured in over 20% of Nobel Prizes.

The world's Jewish population peaked at about fifteen million before the Second World War. Then came the holocaust; where Nazi Germany's 'Final Solution' led to the slaughter of about six million Jews. This is over a third of the Worlds Jewish population. It was not limited to Germany but included their allies and conquered people ranging from Poland to France and into Romania.

Partly because of the holocaust there started a battle to give the remaining Jews a home land which they could identify with. Palestine was then under British rule. The Jews had a cause to fight for but the British had none and very soon they were granted the State of Israel of in May of 1948; internationally recognised by most of the world.

This started a mass immigration to the Promised Land. There were only about 800,000 inhabitants at the time of Israel independence. This rose from about two million by 1958 and is continuing until the present day. There is a large contingent of Ethiopian Jews who were air lifted to Israel in the late 1980's. There is a large contingent of Soviet Jews as well as minorities from Europe and Latin America.

Most Jews speak Hebrew as well as another language. The other language can vary, depending on where they migrated from. The original Jews who where there when they were fighting against the British spoke Arabic as well as Hebrew. Some of the most recent immigrants still maintained their Hebrew language but it has become distorted in time. There is an incredible mixture of languages in a very small country.

There is also an incredible mixture of politics. They range from the Haredi or ultra orthodox Jews to the Hilonim Jewish communities who live a secular lifestyle.

Some of this incredible mix has passed on to Jewish communities throughout the world including the UK. They have their orthodox Jews ranging to those, that I know personally, who will not turn their noses up to a bacon butty if they get the chance.

The reason why the US has the second highest population of Jews goes back to the late eighteen eighties where the Old Russian Empire had its own program of organised persecution of Jews. It was not quite as bad as the holocaust but the term pogrom will have a meaning for all Jews. It is estimated that about two million Jews immigrated to the US before the Revolution which started in 1917 but it was many years before it ended. The few that remained now find that they can have a better standard of living in Israel.

Today Jewish communities throughout the world have a system of Rabbi, a religious leader, a Synagogue and a meeting place. The latter is a place were 'deals are done'. The Synagogue is a place of worship but also acts as a charitable organisation together with the meeting place. If a Jew has fallen on bad times such as losing their job they will immediately turn to their own communities rather than seek government assistance. They will pay for schooling of people who have suffered bereavement. They will also support their elderly. They will also raise funds to pay for this expenditure with each contributing what they can afford. In the US the charitable causes can extend to raising money for Israel.

Today it is clear that Israel will not give up on what it has achieved. It is equally clear that this has been achieved by dispersing a population that was already there. There are plenty of examples where war has meant a realignment of national boundaries. In the war against the Mexicans it was a close thing in the famous 'Alamo' war against the US. If it had gone the other way a large part of Texas, New Mexico and California would now belong to Mexico.

The West Bank was won by war which was not of Israel's making. There will need to be some relocation of Palestinians who were already there. They could instantly be reallocated to another area of Palestinian control using the money which Saudi and the Gulf states continuously spend in lavish living and trying to establish 'a ski- slope' in the desert or a haven for football in the midday sun. Only a fraction of this would leave the Palestinians very suitably compensated.

But is any compensation enough; when your family have been farming these lands for past generations, and then there is the dead. They should be very suitably compensated for what they have lost.

The Israelis do not do themselves any favours in this respect. They want the cheap labour from over the wall they have built; as a security measure. This can take Palestinians as long as a full working day; which doubles the day that they spend away from home. If the Israelis do not wish to take advantage of cheap labour they should provide their own. (Again this comes down to adequate compensation by the Arab states so that the Palestinians can farm their own lands.)

The Christians

The Christians are losing their power except in localities within national boundaries. The once powerful dominant Catholic Church in Rome as in Ireland is losing its grip. My first wife was born in Ireland and was brought up with five children in the UK. I classed them as Convenience Catholics; they did what the priest said in some things and ignored them in others. When they married they decided that they would plan their families as they wished using modern methods of birth control.

The unnatural world of parish priests had finally come out despite all attempts by bishops to thwart them by moving them on to another diocese or retiring them. When I was young I always thought that it was a joke until I met someone at University who had been brought up in a strict Catholic School were many of the tutors were priests. He assured me that it was no joke and he could not wait to leave and became anti Catholic as soon as he left.

More recently, before the general publicity about what had been going on with young men in Catholic institutions there was a documentary on the BBC entitled "The Magdalene Sisters". It featured three women who had suffered endless abuse until 1996 when it came to an end. The laundry featured in the film was run by Nuns. They had such high and mighty titles of "Sisters of Our Lady of Charity", "Sisters of Mercy" or "Sisters of the Good Shepherd".

But there was no charity, strictly the girls had to be paid for their labour but they never were paid. Any wages went straight to running the establishment or into the Nun's pockets. This 'charitable' organisation catered for 'fallen women'. One of the youngest ones was only twelve when her father died and her mother remarried on the condition that Maureen Sullivan did not come with them. She remembers being hidden in a tunnel if school inspectors came. The more conventional ones had just had sex before marriage and if the father was unknown or perhaps there has been incest in the family their parish priest knew just were he could send her to. Once they were inside they never saw any friends or relatives again.

They lived a life of labour and contemplation of their sins. They even had their Christian name changed to anything that the nuns thought more suitable. Anyone who tried to escape could find no one who would help them. The local Garda (the police) did not want to know and if anyone reported a missing person they took them straight back to the nunnery where they were severely punished.

When the Sisters of Our Lady of Charity sold off part of the nunnery to a real-estate developer in 1993 the remains of 155 inmates who had been buried in unmarked graves were found.

On the fifth of February in 2013 Edna Kenny, the Irish prime minister, apologised for the people who had been affected but the few women who survived are still waiting for some compensation.

The Catholic faith is suffering another battering in Spain. There are now estimated to be up to 300,000 babies issued with false identities during and after the Civil war when General Franco came to power. (With Hitler and Mussolini providing air cover and the British government doing nothing to help the legally elected government.)

It was a secret network of doctors, nurses, priests and nuns. It was of course aimed at General Franco's opposition. Ladies who became pregnant were immediately offered the services of a doctor and nurse. (Particularly those who became pregnant and their father had died in the war). They were offered the best of treatment until it was time to give birth. Then they were told that the child had died during or soon after birth. The babies were then passed on to "politically stable" parents who wanted to adopt a child.

But this carried on into 1991, well after General Franco had died. The Catholics were on to a money spinner and the children were offered to the highest bidder. The prices went up as soon as they were limited to the normal lady who might have become pregnant when she was a school or university and could not afford a child at that stage in her career. Many mothers wanted to know who the adoptive parents were; so that they could later see them, but always they were told that the child perished during birth.

Now that the scandal has been revealed, by such journalists as Katy Alder, and gene tests are available some Spaniards are looking for their roots. Some sensible parents told them that they were adopted but others had brought them up as their own only to realise later in life that their offspring did not share any family characteristics.

Up to World War Two the majority of Germans were Catholic including Hitler and many of those who trusted him. It is easy to say that the holocaust was just passed down and ever one else was "just obeying orders" but some were more enthusiastic than Hitler.

The Catholic Church knew exactly what was going on with a confessional system to rival any in the world in intelligence gathering. The Pope at that time was Pope Pius X11. Despite his hearing of confessions as to what was going on via his priests and those below him in Germany, he did nothing. An Excommunication right at the start of those involved in the holocaust would have made many Germans who knew, they could not go on with commands against God's wishes. And thus question Hitler's commands. The amount of anti-Semitic literature poured out by the mass media before the war would have been ample justification that they would be doing God's work in elimination of the Jews. "They killed Our Lord "and the Pope approved.

After the war ended the same pope was there and must have approved of the Nazi escape routes organised by the Catholic Church. There was nothing so dramatic such as the "last U boat" which the allies could have easily dealt with. The safe passages were through neutral countries and carried out one at a time. The escape routes were via Spain and Ireland. They were carried out by 'trusted' servants of Rome and once there they were safe until a passage could be arranged on a neutral ship bound for South America. They had time to change their appearances so they would go undetected.

Shocking as the holocaust was for those troops who first saw the liberation of the few Jews who survived, the higher command of the US, Soviet and UK had other agendas to pursue. They wanted the engineers and scientists who made it all possible. Mainly the US, because they were now so close to perfecting the atom bomb which was soon to end the war in the Pacific.

The recent Pope appeared to carry out an exorcism during one of his masses. There were claims and denials by the Vatican officials organising the mass. What did emerge is that they still believe in this ritual, and even have 'Vatican-approved exorcists' such as Jose Antonia Fortea.

The UK had only one representative, Keith O'Brien, in the recent conclave to choose a new Pope. He declined to attend and later resigned for "sexual misconduct". Elsewhere in the UK the age profile of priests is a growing concern with young men not replacing them!

The Catholic Church still stick to their story of cannibalism when it comes to taking the sacraments. They are told to believe that the wine and bread is transformed to the blood and flesh of Christ.

The congregations are becoming better educated and the last thing the Catholic Church requires is people to question what they are being taught. They only ask blind obedience and their hierarchy can, and should be, believed.

The Muslims

Since the days when Muhammad first introduced Islam it is a fact that **more Muslims have been killed by fellow Muslims than have been killed in combat or by innocent bystanders than all the other non Muslim nations put together**. Today I saw in the paper 86 killed in Iraq and it barely covered about two inches of a report (21/5/2013). The Sunnis were responsible; protesting against the Shia-led government. The attacks featured markets and crowded bus stops – just innocent civilians.

Later that week (23/5/2013) we had another of a series of Muslim attacks in the UK. This time the attacks were carried out by two men in Woolwich Barracks in South London who hacked their victim's body to pieces with a meat cleaver in broad daylight. The victim was only identified by his 'Help for Heroes T shirt'. Drummer Lee Rigby was off duty when it happened.

One of the Muslims was Michael Abebolajo, a Nigerian with a Christening upbringing, who did not become a Muslim until his late teens; he is now 28. It was he who gave a speech after the murder "An eye for an eye, a tooth for a tooth and we won't stop fighting until you leave us alone." The "leave us alone" was referring to the UK troops in Afghanistan and elsewhere. I wonder if he heard what I had read earlier in the week. In Iraq there were far more killed in the latest Sunni and Shia encounter than there have been in Afghanistan for a long time.

It emerged over the next few weeks in the press that Abebolajo's accomplice of 22 has been known to the intelligence services for some time. Both men volunteered for service in North Africa but were stopped and turned back. Then began the 'blame game'; it always goes on in situations such as this. I sympathise with the intelligence services which always have to tread a difficult path between safety of the public and not upsetting minority interests.

One good thing that came out of this incident was the genuine revulsion of the Muslim community. They were keen to point out that their interpretation of the Koran was different from the militants. Perhaps they should produce their own literature instead of relying on Saudi Arabia. They should also be more likely to report suspected militant activities.

A lot of fundamentals remain; one is the theory that a Muslin convert can never switch to another religion; that is punishable by death. Our own Muslim community should make it clear that in a 'free society' an individual can change his mind about what he believes in.

Another is the dream that Muslims can take over the world and then there will be 'peace'. They should just accept that they are living in a free society and they must respect others to see things differently.

Some Muslim practices are illegal in this country. If a Muslim woman is circumcised before she settled in the UK it is beyond our control, but if a family who has settled here tries to do the same to these children it does not matter where it takes place. The child is now under UK protection. If it takes place locally or by sending a child back to relatives in a Muslim country it makes no difference. I recommend any reader who is not familiar with the gory details of how the operation is carried out to look it up on the internet. It stays with the girl for the rest of her life. If a Muslim woman wants to stay permanently in the UK she should undergo a medical examination which should determine whether she has been circumcised. If she has had it done she should be made to swear on the Koran that she will never allow a child in her care to suffer such primitive butchery. I think that most women would welcome this as it is carried out under male pressure.

Muslims should be taught to respect our women. It is not unusual for a woman to wear a bikini in a park or on a beach. They can also be revealing at night in a pub or in a nightclub. This is the norm and women can be free to dress as they like in our free society. Sometimes I fear from them catching hypothermia but some Muslim males interpret it as 'easy meat'. There were eight Muslim males in Rochdale near Manchester who viewed them in this way.

Most of the girls were under the age of consent and living in 'care' accommodation. One young girl said that she had been picked up by a taxi driver and taken to the home of one of them. There she was plied with fags and alcohol until she did not know what she was doing; she was barely thirteen at the time. This carried on from 2008 until May 2012 during which time more and more girls were added to their list. They used extreme violence to keep their personal harem where they could do whatever they liked. I emphasise that eight men took part in this and have now been named; the only girls where white. I shudder to think of what might be going on in other parts of the country. Some of the men lived 'conventional' lives with women and children of their own but they would be horrified if any of their own women was treated in this way.

Arranged marriages are something which is the norm in Muslim countries. I once remember watching a video of Hamas rewarding their freedom fighters with child brides; some less that ten years old. They would then go back to their fathers who would keep them until puberty. We have a name for this, paedophilia.

Muslim men coming here must accept that they leave all traditions relating the opposite sex behind them. We have even bent over backwards to enable them to introduce Sharia 'law' for Britain. We have laws of our own and all people should obey them.

One of the things Muslims do is 'marriage counselling' but this starts from the assumption that the women must have done something wrong. And she should first go to the husband who beat her. Sharia law in Britain has gone too far and it should cease.

A woman who covers her face in public must be required to remove her veil. It is an obvious security risk and it makes the rest of us feel uneasy.

Above all the Muslim communities here and elsewhere are responsible for an above average birth rate. It is already too high and should be curtailed with a proper Birth Control program.

A Summary of Religion

I will leave this summary to 'Imagine' by John Lennon.

"Nothing to kill or die for, and no religion too."

Religion has been the excuse for killing throughout the ages. Unfortunately it is still with us today. The one hope is that one day enlightenment will sweep the world; but perhaps I am a 'dreamer'.

DRUGS

The only drugs which have had a significant impact on my life are nicotine and alcohol. I have occasionally tried cannabis and may well try other drugs before I die.

I first started drinking when I was fourteen and had my first ten pint session before I was sixteen. My capacity had decreased significantly with age but I still find it to be the ideal social drug and I have no regrets.

In my early teens I made a conscious decision never to smoke. This was at a time when the overwhelming majority of adults did smoke, including all those in my family, and friends in my own age group had already started. I first started to smoke in my mid thirties when my first marriage was breaking up. I have smoked ever since except for brief intervals when I was trying to kick the habit.

Any thought of giving up smoking ended in July 2007 when the government decreed that I had to give up or forfeit my social life. My hackles always rise whenever I am told not to do something without any sound convincing reasons as to why I should. This topic is covered in detail later in this chapter.

Overview of Drugs

There are two distinct dictionary definitions of the word drug. The first one is "any natural or synthetic substance used to treat or prevent a disease or ailment". The second one is "any natural or synthetic substance taken for the pleasant effects it produces". The latter definition applies to most of this chapter and drugs used in this way are often referred to as recreational drugs. A potential problem with recreational drugs is that **some** of them can lead **some** individuals to become dependent on them.

I have never heard of or read about any society that did not have any recreational drugs that were not perfectly acceptable and legal. Today there are some societies where one drug is a taboo in one country but perfectly legal and acceptable in other countries. There are even countries where a drug is acceptable in one state or area but not in another.

In the UK there is there is currently a system of classification of illegal drugs which is as follows;

Class A: Ecstasy, LSD, Heroin, Cocaine, Crack Cocaine, Magic Mushrooms, Methadone, Meth Amphetamine (Crystal Meth), and any Class B drug, e.g. amphetamine, if prepared for injection.

Class B: Amphetamines, Cannabis, Codeine, Methylphenidate (Ritalin), and Pholcodine.

Class C: Tranquilisers, Some painkillers, Gamma Hydroxbutyrate (GHB), and Ketamine.

There are two key questions about taking a recreational drug:

1. How does taking the drug affect me/the person taking it?

2. How does me/another individual taking the drug affect other members of society?

After many years pondering over these questions I now firmly believe that taking recreational drugs should be a personal choice and there should be no legislation against taking any of them.

Any legislation against taking any drug immediately raises two further issues:

(1)   Is it effective in reducing the use of the drug?

(2)   What effect does the legislation have on other members of society?

For many years now successive governments have had 'hard line' policies against drugs, particularly those in class A. Police forces have followed the government directive and introduced 'zero tolerance' policies on their patches. They have made sufficient arrests to clog up the courts and gaols, and keep an army of lawyers fully occupied.

What might have happened without all the government and police 'initiatives' we will never know. **What we do know is that during this time there has been a steady increase in the supply and demand for illegal drugs**. The prices of some illegal drugs are actually falling whilst the price of legal drugs such as tobacco and alcohol continues to rise. **A fiscally aware youngster who naturally wants a 'good feeling' on a night out may well decide that an illegal drug offers better value for money than a legal one.** The present policies are clearly not reducing the use of illegal drugs; surely it is time to look at alternative approaches?

Making drugs illegal has an impact on other members of society who never take them particularly for people of my generation. The minority of illegal drug takers who become addicted and dependant on a drug need a regular supply. If they have no money to buy them with they will steal money in any way they can. Many of the crimes committed by members of the 'underclass' are generally accepted to be drug related. Every form and level of the media has regular features on some of the most extreme cases where someone dies, is crippled or suffers horrific facial injuries. Often the amount of money taken is relatively small, such as an elderly person's weekly pension but it is sufficient to keep the drug addict going until they run out again. There have always been thefts and muggings but I cannot remember a time when they have been as vicious as they are today. Clearly the people carrying out such attacks are desperate and deranged at the time of the attacks.

Any drug sold 'on the street' has to have a chain of supply since many of the illegal drugs are grown or manufactured in distant countries. These supplies are controlled by gangs who can make a very good living from it. Territorial wars break out when gangs clash in 'turf wars'. In some cases these may just result in beatings and injuries which the NHS has to deal with. In some extreme cases innocent bystanders may be killed during a gangland shootout.

The current government policies on illegal drugs are clearly affecting many innocent people and should be reviewed.

Before looking at the consequences of my suggestion of **legalising all drugs** it is worthwhile looking at some of the individual drugs.

The Opiates

Opium is a natural drug produced from the flowers of the opium poppy. Ancient Egyptian doctors used it to relieved pain by getting the patient to eat poppy seeds. Modern doctors use morphine and codeine which are derived from the poppy seeds.

Heroin is a synthesized drug which requires the addition of chemicals to the morphine from the poppy. In its purest form it has a white crystalline structure but this is normally diluted with other compounds to form a white powder before being used. It produces a feeling of relaxation and euphoria. It can be taken orally but the effects are much quicker and intense when injected directly into a vein.

The most natural way to use opium for relaxation is to smoke it. The opium is extracted from unripe seed pods by making a series of cuts and collecting the milky resin which drips from the pod in a similar way that latex is extracted from rubber trees. Although it starts off white it hardens to a brownish gum. The ideal way to smoke it is then in a sophisticated design of pipe which slowly heats up the gum without setting it on fire whilst the fumes are inhaled.

A very good friend of mine, the late Ashok Bannerjee, often talked about his father who was a doctor in what was once a small village on the outskirts of Calcutta that is now part of the urban sprawl of present day Kolkata. He was the only doctor in the area and they had no NHS. Those who could afford his services paid his fees in rupees, those with no money gave him a chicken, a few eggs or a basket of fruit and vegetables. They ate well and any excess food was passed on to the poor in the village. Although he drank both wine and beer in moderation, at the end of the day his favourite drug was opium which he smoked last thing at night before going to bed. He was in an ideal position to assess the use of drugs in his area and their impact on society. He was a very active man who never fully retired and lived until he was 91. His single pipe of opium each day does not seem to have done him much harm.

If I ever got the chance I would certainly try a pipe of opium but I doubt if I will ever understand how anyone can inject themselves with heroin. They are both class A drugs.

Cocaine

Cocaine is another natural drug which is produced in the leaves of the coca bush which grows in the mountainous regions of the northern part of South America, mainly in Bolivia and Peru. The locals there have been chewing the leaves to extract the cocaine for centuries. They do not use the drug simply for recreational purposes; they use it throughout the day to help them through arduous working days toiling in the hills or in the mines at altitudes which very few people could work in.

Cocaine was only introduced to the rest of the world in the 1800's although the Spaniards had observed its use in the 1600's. Pure cocaine was extracted from the leaves of the coca plant in 1860 in Europe and was used in medicinal and consumer products. It was used as an anaesthetic for eye, nose and throat surgery and the psychologist Sigmund Freud used it to treat depression. The brand name soft drink Coca-Cola was named in 1885 after the coca leaf extract it contained and was originally marketed as a medical elixir. I often wonder if one of the 'secret special ingredients' of today's drink is still a trace of coke. It might account for how some people seen to be addicted to the foul tasting stuff.

The modern recreational drug is chemically prepared as either a powdered hydrochloride salt or as a rock crystal. The powdered form is normally either snorted so that it is absorbed by the nasal tissues or dissolved in water and injected. It may also be smoked. The rock crystal form is heated to produce vapours which are then smoked and absorbed in the lungs. The heating produces a crackling noise from which the term' crack cocaine' is derived.

I know people who have occasionally snorted cocaine powder on 'special occasions' and they do not seem to be any the worse for it. Regular use of any form of pure cocaine can very easily lead to problems and dependency. Along with heroin it is one of the most dangerous drugs on the market.

The only form of cocaine I have ever tried is chewing the leaves. I once went on a guided tour of some botanical gardens in the Far East. There were several bushes and one of them had plenty of leaves. I have to confess that I pinched a few which I tried later that day. I did not notice any effect. I had wanted to try them ever since I had a first hand report from an old friend and colleague from my teaching days. Joe Powell was one of the most interesting characters I have ever met. Being a German he was interned at the start of the First World War but the authorities soon realised that he was more anti the Hitler regime than the average Brit. He finished up being trained as a sniper who operated behind the enemy lines. He spent all of one long summer vacation in the Andes. He did the usual tourist trips but then spent some time at a small village which he used as a base for walking. The locals soon introduced him to chewing the leaf of the coca bush. After trying it for the first time he never went walking without some leaves as well as his lunch and water. He had no withdrawal symptoms when he returned to the UK. If I ever go there I will certainly try some.

Ecstasy

Ecstasy is a chemical compound which was first synthesised in Germany in 1912 when it was known as MDMA (an abbreviation of the chemical composition) but it only started to be used as a recreational drug in the 1970's and was given a class A classification in 1977. It is normally taken as a tablet.

It is often taken at 'music' parties which have become known as raves. It seems to be the ideal drug for such occasions because a tablet can take up to an hour to have any effect and then reaches a plateau which can last for up to three hours. During this time people seem to have not only the urge but the stamina to keep on dancing for long periods of time, far longer than they would without the drug.

The users report an intensification of their senses: hearing, vision, smell, touch and taste. They feel empathy and compassion to other people and freely mix with people they have never met before. They also find that they can openly discuss topics which normally they would prefer not to.

The down sides to taking ecstasy may take place late in the evening or more likely the following morning. Users can feel totally shattered with lots of muscular aches and pains. The former reminds me of a hangover after having too much alcohol and the latter of having too much exercise after a layoff.

The main dangers in taking ecstasy seem to be mixing it with other drugs, dehydration from not taking sufficient fluids to replace the perspiration losses during the dancing or taking too much of it in search of an even higher high.

In 1985 the street price of a tablet of ecstasy was about £25; today it may be as little as £5 so it is easy to see how attractive it can be to young people. The fact that it is a 'young persons' drug is born out by a survey of 500 students at Edinburgh University in 2005; 36% admitted to having taken it and, of those who had, 75% described it as having a 'positive force' on their lives. I suspect that a survey taken today would result in even higher figures.

I first thought seriously about ecstasy when I read about a young girl dying after taking it. The report also included an account of its widespread usage and other people who had died from taking it. I soon reasoned that the number of deaths was incredibly small compared with deaths from using other drugs and activities where drugs are not involved. During my time in academia there was a sad case of one of our students dying during a football match but that was of no interest to the national media.

Since researching the subject I have found out that most deaths associated with taking ecstasy are a combination of factors and taking the drug may not be the major one.

One of these is heatstroke. Intensive activity in a hot and humid atmosphere is always likely to increase the body temperature above its norm of about 37°C and the danger limit is only 40°C. Marathon runners face the same potential problem in warm climates.

Another one is taking too little fluid and in some cases too much by people very aware of the consequences of taking too little and overdoing it. Too little can result in dehydration and too much can result in dilutional hyponaetremia.

The final factor is an undiagnosed medical condition; usually a heart problem. The student I mentioned earlier could just as easily have died at a rave party as he did on a football pitch.

The above causes of death all assume a pure tablet has been taken. As with any uncontrolled drug there are invariably some batches which reach the market with impurities. This was the probably the cause of the only case I could find of two fatalities during the same event.

Ecstasy is currently undergoing clinical trials for its therapeutic properties in treating patients with post-traumatic stress disorder.

I am very unlikely ever to go to a rave party but in the right setting I might give ecstasy a try provided I was confident that the tablet had not been contaminated.

Magic Mushrooms

The fly agaric is an eye-catching fungus with a bright red cap speckled with white spots mounted above a white stem. They are not uncommon in the UK; there is a wood about a mile from where I live where they appear most years and I once saw some fine specimens in a London park. The first time I saw a picture of one was as a child. In those days they often featured in children's books; I expect that will have changed now.

I regularly collect edible fungi and prefer to limit the term mushroom to the common field and horse mushrooms or the cultivated varieties from the shops but the term "magic mushroom" is well established and applies to any fungi which produces hallucinogenic drugs such as psilocybin.

Our native fly agaric is one of the less potent varieties of magic mushroom. Worldwide there are hundreds of varieties of magic mushrooms and people who take them regularly are more likely to be using fungi which are endemic in Mexico or Thailand. They are now often cultivated in other countries such as Holland, as they once were in the UK until 2005.

Magic mushrooms are the most natural of drugs and references have been made to them throughout recorded history. There are some people who would go back even further by claiming that some cave drawings from 9,000 years ago are illustrations of magic mushrooms. They have certainly been used in the pre-Christian era during religious ceremonies in countries as far apart as Mexico, Ireland and Russia, and are no doubt still used in this way by minority sects in some countries.

Magic mushrooms can be eaten raw or after they have been dried. The drying process allows for them to be stored and produces a much stronger drug by weight but just the same in terms of the number of mushrooms.

Users of fresh mushrooms experience effects including giggling fits and intensification of colours, lights and sounds and sometimes hallucinations. The negative effects can include vomiting, and anxiety.

Prior to 2005 the UK had a strange law which did not forbid eating fresh magic mushrooms but banned the eating of dried ones. If they had been' half dried' by leaving them out in the sun for a while our lawyers could have costly 'half baked' arguments on the definition of the term 'dry'. In 2005 the government cleared this up by deciding on a complete ban and give all forms of magic mushrooms a category A classification. I suppose their motive was to make them look 'tough on drugs' but to many it just made them look stupid.

I have a close relative who once went on a fly agaric 'trip'. I asked him what it was like. He said that he had no idea because he probably ate too many and did not remember a thing about it; not a very successful trip from his point of view. However the friends he was with were entertained for a long time by some of the antics he got up to and told him all about it the next day.

This is another drug which I might try some day but it would have to be in the right company which included someone who was knowledgeable about how many to eat, bearing in mind that they can vary quite a lot in size.

LSD

LSD is a powerful hallucinogenic drug named after the molecules in the compound. It was first synthesised in 1938 by the Swiss chemist, Albert Hoffman, who was interested in developing medicines from compounds in *ergot*, a fungus that attacks rye. Soon after his discovery he had to work on other projects and only returned to his LSD project in 1944 when he decided to experiment on himself.

In his first experiment he described feelings of dizziness, anxiety, visual distortions and a desire to laugh. After another experiment in his laboratory he asked an assistant to take him home. When they somehow managed to get to his home by bicycle he asked the lady who lived next door for some milk and while he was drinking it wrote down that "She no longer looked like Mrs R, but a rather malevolent, insidious witch with a coloured mask."

In 1947 LSD was first produced commercially by Sandoz under the trade name Delvsid as a therapeutic drug for use in psychiatric treatments. In the 1950's the American CIA set up a program to test the drug on students and servicemen because they saw a potential for its use in interrogations and mind control.

By the 1960's it had started to be used as a recreational drug particularly by entertainers and artists. One of The Beatles' songs, 'Lucy in the sky with diamonds', allegedly describes an LSD trip.

It increased in popularity until 1977 when the police found the laboratory where most of the UK supply originated in Tregaron in mid-Wales. The price rocketed and the consumption fell to very low levels. Research on potential therapeutic uses of LSD had already been abandoned for political reasons. There has already been a rethink on the medicinal uses of LSD and a reanalysis of data taken before it was banned in most countries shows that it was more effective in treating alcoholism than the more socially acceptable help groups.

LSD is a relatively none addictive drug and if the effect of taking it has inspired some people to create works of art as some of them claim it does there is a case for using it. However the downside that some people imagine that they can fly during a trip may not cause too many problems in a bungalow or a tent but can be, and often is fatal when taken in a tall building.

I think that LSD is one drug I would give a miss if ever I was offered the chance to try some.

Cannabis

This is a drug which I do know something about from talking with friends and acquaintances and, unlike many of our leading politicians, I admit to taking it myself on more than one occasion and not "only once, at a party when I was a student". In fact when I was a student not only did I not try it but I never came across anyone who had – I suppose that dates me a bit or is just a consequence of spending so much of my time on academic work, sports, politics and earning enough money to support a family which left very little time for parties.

Cannabis is present in all parts of a plant from the same family as the hop plant used in brewing. The active ingredient is a chemical compound (which is abbreviated to THC for people without a degree in chemistry) and the concentration of THC determines the strength of the drug.

There are at least three varieties of the cannabis plant which are endemic to some areas of the world. The oldest well documented use of the drug came from the grave of a shaman in a remote region of China which was estimated to be 2,700 years old. Among the well preserved remains was a bowl filled with over 0.75 kg of dried cannabis plants. It is unclear if it would have been used for medicinal purposes, religious ceremonies or simply as a recreational drug. The plants have now been introduced to most countries and cannabis is by far the most popular 'illegal' drug worldwide.

The simplest way to prepare the plant for smoking is to dry the leaves until they are readily combustible. It can then be smoked in a cigarette paper or pipe with or without diluting it with tobacco. A friend of mine who has smoked it for many years will only use it pure because he is worried about becoming addicted to the tobacco.

It can also be concentrated into a solid lump of brown coloured resin when it is invariably used with tobacco by scraping off small pieces to mix with the tobacco. In this form only a very small volume is need to 'roll a joint' which makes it easy to transport and sell on the street.

Cannabis can also be taken orally in a variety of culinary dishes, the most popular form being cannabis cake. A close relative of mine once had someone staying with them. He was on his own in the house when he felt hungry and helped himself to a slice of cake without knowing what was in it. He liked it so much he had a few more and finally scoffed half of it. By the time the rest of the household returned he was clearly in the middle of a severe trip and needed to be carefully watched until the following morning. On the odd occasions when I go there I always complain that although there is always some delicious home made, low sugar cake with lots of fruit in, I have never had the chance to try a sensible portion of their cake with the special ingredient.

When taken in sensible quantities cannabis produces a feeling of relaxation which releases inhibitions and makes people more talkative and giggly. It can have mild hallucinogenic effects but never the severe effects associated with LSD. Sound and vision can be affected in very interesting and pleasant ways.

I remember being in India with my wife and a good friend and his partner. We were in one of the states where cannabis was illegal but Roger had still managed to buy sufficient leaves for a few joints. We were outside a bar in the grounds of one of the hotels which was one of the few places that alcohol was tolerated. Both the ladies decided to stick to the expensive white wine while Roger and I had a few joints with our beer. We were feeling pleasantly relaxed, as we would have been anyway, and when my wife enquired about the effects of the joint I responded "not a lot". Then I leaned back to observe the sky and the setting sun. I have often observed spectacular sunrises and sunsets in different parts of the world but this time I realised that there was something different about that one. There was a distinct green arc among some of the usual colours. When I pointed this out to the rest of the company I was the only one who could see it!

I was staying with some friends who were regular users the first time I tried cannabis. I tried it the first night I was there. It was an exhausting day and it did not seem to have much effect and I was soon ready for bed. I tried it again the following evening when I had more time and it certainly did. We had an ancient tape or record player on providing some background music. Suddenly I realised that the sounds I was listening to were more distinct than those I had heard from the most modern complex stereo systems available. Not only that, but the pace seemed to be slowed down so that I could identify individual instruments and hear things which had previously been part of a blurred background. That was a very pleasant and illuminating experience.

I once had an equally illuminating but not entirely pleasant experience with cannabis while I was working in Holland. I was having a beer in a bar when I noticed that they had a 'menu' with a selection of joints. They varied in price depending on the 'strength'. I asked for one of the strongest ones. It quickly had some effect and I was soon enjoying the enhancement of the background music. I then foolishly had another one. The pleasurable effects did not increase but I suddenly became very hungry and I started to consume several plates of mixed nuts. I later found out that this is a common reaction known as the 'munchies'.

I then decided to move to a different position at the bar in the hope of joining in some of the conversation that was taking place at the far end. I suddenly found that I could not move; my lower body seemed to be glued to the bar stool although my upper body was OK. This was not something I had expected. I am not the sort of person who panics or asks for help in unexpected situations so I simply thought through the dilemma I was in. My body was not functioning the way it should and I was in a bar I had never been in before in the back streets of one of the shadier parts of The Hague. I started to order strong coffees instead of beer while carrying on eating the nuts. When I eventually managed to prise my legs from the bar stool I stood at the bar exercising my legs and cautiously moving along it. When I was confident that I could walk again I paid my tab and somehow managed to find Central Station where I caught the sprinter train back to my hotel.

One of the problems with all drugs is that some people are never content to just enjoy a product as it is. Just as horticulturists have achieved some remarkable changes in the fruit and vegetables we eat they have made significant changes to the original cannabis plants. Selective breeding programs have been undertaken for some time now with the aim of producing plants with higher and higher concentrations of THC. These plants are now know as "skunk" cannabis plants; the strong concentration of THC being analogous to the strong smell of the animal with the same name. I am still not sure if it was skunk I tried in the 1990s but what I did try was strong enough to be sensibly limited to a single joint. If I had been with someone with local knowledge I would probably have been advised to try one of the less potent ones.

Skunk has certainly increased in potency in recent years and anyone trying it should be very cautious. Negative experiences feed the media and government cases for having all forms of cannabis banned.

At the time or writing cannabis is controversially a class B drug. There are some people who would like to see it in class A and others who would like to see it declassified.

According to the web site Police999.com there have been no reported deaths in the UK from an overdose of cannabis. There have no doubt been cases where people have died after taking cannabis. After my strange trip in The Hague I might have stepped under the train back to the hotel instead of into it but the cause of death would have been destruction of major organs by the wheel of a train. The web site I have just quoted is a very interesting one. It is not connected to any official police organisation and is manned by people who have served in the force but are now retired or in other occupations and serving officers who have views they want to air when 'official channels' have not been interested.

The medical benefits of cannabis now seem to be widely accepted although not always acceptable. I have met two ladies who both swear that cannabis is the only drug which relieves their medical problems. One had tried a variety of prescription drugs over a long period of time before someone suggested that she tried cannabis.

I have used cannabis on several occasions since my experience in Holland and will continue to do so whenever I get the chance. I would of course be very cautious and confident of my company and surroundings before trying skunk.

Legal Drugs

When the word drugs is mentioned to most people they immediately think in terms of illegal drugs and yet some of the most addictive and dangerous drugs are perfectly legal in the UK.

Prescription Drugs

On May 2nd 2012 the Daily Telegraph had a sensation seeking headline on the front page "Lethal errors in 2m prescriptions". Anyone who actually took the trouble to read the article found that it was based on a twelve month analysis of 1,700 patients in just 15 medical practices and one in 550 prescriptions had what they described as a 'severe error'. One of the severe errors they identified was wrongly prescribed warfarin which is a blood thinning agent and more commonly used in rat poison. They did not find any error which had actually resulted in a death, which is what I understand 'lethal' means.

There is seldom a day when most of the national press do not have an article finding faults with either a medical practitioner or a hospital. They love 'league tables' because someone or some organisation must be bottom and they can have a go at them. Building up the public's expectations for a system where nobody makes any mistakes is ridiculous.

My main concern with the health service is how dependant people can become on prescription drugs and pain relief treatments from a chemist. I know that in some cases one drug will be prescribed to alleviate the symptoms of another one so that the total number can escalate. In the years leading up to her death my mother was taking so many that she rattled when she walked. Now I find many people of my age group doing the same.

Overdoses of prescription drugs results in many deaths. In a minority of cases this may be intentional; in most cases it is due to inadvertently taking more than has been prescribed. It would be interesting to know how these compare with the figures for deaths from illegal drugs.

Caffeine

If someone had told anyone of my parent's generation that they were taking a drug when they were drinking one their many cups of tea a day they would have thought the idea to be preposterous and anyone saying it crazy.

Research has shown that the caffeine in tea, coffee or chocolate not only stimulates the brain but increases the heart rate. Many years ago I was once found to be marginal on the latter while undergoing a few basic tests to attend a gym. This meant that they would need a medical from a doctor before I could start. I explained that I had recently been using another gym with no problems. I was asked what I had been doing prior to the test. I had just finished a coffee and a cigar while I was waiting for them to open. I came back the next day to repeat the same test without any coffee or nicotine as they suggested. I was told that the new reading was typical for someone half my age.

Ever since then I have always made it a rule to have no coffee or cigar for at least an hour before a medical and to throw in a few yoga breathing exercises for good measure. A few weeks ago, in my 74th year, I had no problem passing my scuba diving medical which is far more rigorous than the gym test was.

The effect caffeine has on the heart rate led to it getting a very bad press and caffeine- free coffee became a fad. I could never see the point of this no more than I could see the point of alcohol free beer. Extra processing is required for both which increases the cost and I would sooner drink hot water than de-caffeinated coffee.

Is increasing the heart rate for a while such a bad thing? I deliberately do it regularly when I am exercising; and my old brain needs stimulation to produce its best work output.

As with many contentious drugs 'experts' advice can change from week to week. Yesterday I read that up to 4 cups of coffee a day is good for you; last week I read that any amount is bad for you. I will carry on starting my usual day at about 4.00 a.m. drinking nothing except coffee with a few cigars until the papers arrive and it is time for breakfast. I always find these to be my most 'creative hours'.

Alcohol

Alcohol is the most natural of all drugs. Whenever any form of sugar is in contact with a liquid and a yeast alcohol will be produced.

It would have been used by animals long before the evolution of the human race. Most varieties of fruit contain their own yeast and rotting provides sufficient liquid to produce alcohol. In the UK any animal such as a horse or pig can show symptoms of drunkenness after eating windfalls in an orchard in the autumn but the most spectacular examples have recently been demonstrated in wildlife documentaries showing monkeys and elephants change their behaviour after gorging on rotting fruit. Their experience is passed on down through the troop or herd and they regularly return to the same location for an annual binge.

Alcohol has been intentionally produced by most societies since the beginning of recorded time and probably long before that. Historians are no doubt correct to assume that each society discovered alcohol accidentally. I can add something to that from my own experience. During 'vacations' when I was about 15 I worked for a company in Chorley, Lancashire which produced a variety of soft drinks. One of their products was fruit cordials and occasionally a bottle was returned from a customer because it had 'gone off'. I naturally enquired 'why?' because it seemed such a waste of their most expensive line. I was informed that it was because it had started to ferment and I did not have to worry about it being wasted. It was the chief chemist's favourite tipple.

Alcohol has been used for medicinal purposes, a source of nutrients and as a central feature of religious rites as well as for pleasure for many years. The ancient Egyptians had many types of beer and wine and Osiris, their god of wine, was one of their most powerful gods. Wine is still regarded as an essential feature of key religious ceremonies by most of today's Christian sects.

The alcoholic content is now universally measured by the percentage of ethanol/ethyl alcohol by volume which is abbreviated to ABV.

Alcoholic drinks can be broadly classified as follows:

Beers

Beers, ales, stouts, and ciders are all included in this section. They are categorised by having a relatively low alcohol content of between 2.5% and 6% alcohol by volume which is now abbreviated to ABV.

In the brewing process the source of the glucose/sugar are the starches derived from cereal grains. In the UK we use malted barley (barley which is just starting to germinate) but worldwide wheat, corn (maize) and rice are used. Hops which give the drink a pleasant bitter flavour are in most of them and each product will use a specific strain of yeast and hops. Other ingredients may be added to give a distinctive texture and flavour.

Cider is the odd ball in this list since the sugar is in the juice of pressed apples and the question as to whether is should be classed as a weak wine, makes an interesting bar room discussion.

Wines

Most commercial wines are made from grape juice with the green grape producing white wine and the red grapes red wine. However any enterprising home brewer will tell you that any fruit with a high sugar content can produce wines which are just as good. Elderberry, plum, damson and strawberry are amongst the most popular. To increase the alcohol content additional sugar is normally added. Even flowers can be used but these just provide a flavour and even more sugar is needed. As with beers, different yeasts have been developed for different wines.

Provided the temperature is right, fermentation of any wine mixture will continue until either all the sugar has been used up or the alcohol content reaches about 12%. If all the sugar has been used up it is known as a dry wine and, if there is still some unfermented sugar, a sweet wine.

Spirits

To increase the alcohol content of a drink above that which can be achieved by natural fermentation requires a process called distillation. Alcohol has a lower boiling point than water - about 78°C compared with 100°C. If a mixture of alcohol and water is heated the vapours produced will contain a higher proportion of alcohol than the mixture being heated. These vapours are then condensed by cooling in a heat exchanger. Multiple distillations can be used to produce pure alcohol for non drinking uses such as a fuel for vehicles. The excess production of wine in Europe sometimes produces 'wine lakes' which are disposed of in this way.

The aim of distillation in the drinks industry is to produce a mixture where the alcohol content is sufficient to give the drink a distinctive 'kick' when it is sipped in small quantities.

Most spirits produced commercially have an ABV content of about 40%. The fermented mixtures used to produce the most popular brands of spirits are beer for whisky, wine for brandy, sugar cane for rum and a grain based liquor flavoured with juniper berries for gin.

In the UK before 1980 we classified the strength of spirits by 'proof', a typical value being about 70%. This terminology originated in the British navy in the days when a daily ration of rum was the norm. Unscrupulous captains could make a bit of extra money by watering down the rum just as landlords ashore often did with beer. The sailors developed a procedure to test the rum. Gunpowder was sprinkled on to a sample of the rum and a flame held near the surface. If it ignited that was proof that it had not been watered down. The minimum alcohol content required to sustain combustion is about 57% ABV so this set the standard of 100% proof. Since this was a minimum standard some of the rum they drank would have been more than 100% proof. The older sea dogs who had lived long enough to tell their tales presumably left their tots until they had finished any work in the rigging.

Fortified Wines

These are a mixture of a wine and a spirit. In a port a spirit is added to the base wine to increase the alcohol strength of the drink to about 20% ABV. Sherries have a much lower alcohol content which may be only slightly higher than some wines. They are usually made from a very dry wine with some spirit added.

Pleasures & Dangers of Alcohol

All the men on my mother's side of the family have a long history of alcoholic drinks playing an important part of their lives. My great, great grandfather managed to survive serving in the last of the merchant sailing ships to retire ashore and become the landlord of a pub on the outskirts of Liverpool. I know that my grandfather and both my uncles were the same. On my father's side of the family I have no idea except of course my father himself who seldom missed a day without a visit to a club or pub.

I spent some of my formative years living in a working men's club and then a pub. Alcohol has been an important part of my life ever since. On the positive side it has been central to most of the memorable social occasions in my life; on the negative side I have seen far too many people including some very good friends become alcoholics and lose jobs, relationships, homes and ultimately their lives because of it.

I am therefore in a much better position to offer some guidelines on this subject than most of the 'experts' (often also hypocrites) who base findings on statistics and use sensationalism to ensure maximum media coverage on the negative aspects or drink.

A good night out

There have been so many I will limit this section to my most recent one. Last Friday, 11th May 2012, was the annual reunion of the class of Building Service Engineers who graduated from Wolverhampton University in 1990. Only 16 students graduated that year and one tragically died a few years ago. They all now have senior positions as consultants or heads of NHS or other government organisations; one for example has responsibility for all police buildings in the West Midlands area. Some work in areas remote from the West Midlands but still managed to attend. For example Steve had driven up from Southend in Essex and Adrian had come by train from Aberystwyth in Wales.

I had been the only member of staff to attend these events since the first few but this year Roger, an old student, ex-colleague and still a good friend of mine managed to join us. Altogether there were 11 students and 2 members of staff. The first three to arrive at about 18.30 were Adrian, Roger and me. The evening got off to a good start when Adrian asked Roger where he used to sit in the class. Roger replied that he didn't; he stood at the front! Of course they had not seen each other for over 20 years.

Since the smoking ban we always meet at the Moat House in Birmingham. The building has deep overhangs which provide excellent cover with seating overlooking the canal and Sea World on the opposite bank. It is perfect for the smokers in the group.

There were only two of the group who had to drive home and they limited themselves to a couple of pints and soft drinks. For the rest of us the beer flowed freely all night until the mad dash ending at about 23.00 hours as people left to catch transport home. Our reunions have always been 'boozy do's', in the early days some of the lads would carry on to a nightclub and catch first trains home instead of last ones. Without the relaxing effect of alcohol I am sure we would never have had such great evenings which everyone still makes such an effort to attend each year.

I am certain my life would have been much more mundane if it had been alcohol free.

Individual & racial tolerance to alcohol

I became aware of individuals different attitudes and capacities for drinking beer long before I was technically old enough to drink myself. As well as living in a working men's club I also worked there. There were some members who would be ready for their second pint before I managed to give them their change for the first one. There were others who never had more than three or four pints all night.

After I left home at 17 to become a cadet engineer it was soon clear that some of our group had never drunk before and had a very low tolerance to alcohol while others soon adapted to having a "session" naturally. Of the former group Steve had only had two pints at lunchtime when we returned to Riversdale College. Another student had an open topped car he was showing off to another group. Steve asked if he could sit in it to 'feel what it was like'. The next minute he drove off out of the car park, up the lane past Liverpool Cricket ground towards the main road. I immediately tried to stop him and almost got run over, I then ran after him as he disappeared up the lane. Fortunately he soon came back but then managed to dislodge the flywheel by finding the reverse gear when he was just trying to find a lower gear. Afterwards he said he did not understand why he had done it but he often had only soft drinks and never more than a couple of pints for the rest of the time that I knew him.

Meredith's story had a much worse ending. He had a low tolerance to alcohol but always tried to keep up with anyone he was drinking with and finished up in some sorry states. In the last year of our apprenticeship some of us were in one of the companies' workshops and we found an 'excuse' for a lunchtime session. The pub was behind the workshop and it was a long detour to reach it from the main gate at the front. We only had about five pints when I looked at my watch and realised that it was time to get back. The wall was a high one but there were plenty of hand and footholds in the old brickwork. Most of us were soon back in the workshop and we were only a few minutes late. Later that afternoon we heard that Meredith had been taken to hospital. He had made it to the top of the wall but then landed badly with his face taking some of the impact. A year or so after we had finished our apprenticeships and I was at university I heard that he had committed suicide.

At the other end of the 'drinking scale' Les could drink as much as I could. He once returned from a weekend at home and proudly announced that he had managed 20 pints in one long session. Not to be outdone I managed 22 the following weekend when I was at home and still managed to stagger the two miles back to where my parents were living at the time. Looking back, it was a stupid thing to do. A friend I was with during the last few hours told me I had got to the point where I was no longer enjoying the evening and just had an obsession with numbers. He walked the first half mile back with be until he was confident I was going to make it.

My advice to anyone now is to be aware of their own tolerances at as early an age as possible. Once you know what your limit is likely to be in a particular situation, stick to it, miss out on some rounds and never try and keep up with the 'pace setters'.

Just as some individuals of the same race can have varying reactions to alcohol it is also well established that some races have lower tolerances than others. Most northern European people have been drinking beer for centuries while southern European people have been drinking wine for just as long. Other races had never experienced it until they came in contact with Europeans. The Aborigines of Australia and the North American Indians are extreme examples. As hunter gatherers who often travelled great distances during the year they would not have had much chance to experiment with alcoholic drinks. When they did the results were often sad and disastrous and continue to be a problem for many of them today.

Violence and alcohol

People with similar tolerances to quantities of alcohol can often behave in quite different ways after they have had 'their quota'. The vast majority of people enjoy the effects and the ideal ending to a session is a serious frank discussion or a sing song when even my unmelodious voice can be tolerated. For a very small minority the ideal ending seems to be a fight. This is particularly true of young people although for some it may continue throughout their lives. Once it was the prerogative of men but women are increasingly involved.

I have had my fair share of experiences of violence after drinking. When I lived in licensed premises there were one or two individuals who needed to be humoured and not provoked in any way towards the end of an evening. I once had to help my father in restraining one of them who was subsequently banned from the club.

During the vacation I spent working on an Irish tar gang building the M6 motorway, I found myself in the middle of a fight involving about eight people. I was the only Englishman in the group who went straight to a pub on a Friday night. It had been a great night; we had all had our fill of Guinness and beer and we were still singing as we set off back to where we were lodging. Then this fight started with some of the locals. I was still trying to find out what it was all about when I noticed one of the bigger Irish lads looking like he was going to do serious damage to a much smaller local. I made the mistake of stepping in between them to stop it. This left me defenceless against the punch I never saw coming from another local and I still have a small scar along my right eyebrow from that night.

On Monday when we were all back at work, the fight was the only topic of conversation during our brief breaks. Most of the Irish were proud to relate their contributions and used inane terminology like 'a good fight' and the one who had not been with us regretted his absence. I tried in vain to find out what it had all been about but no one was sure. "The big one said something as we were leaving" was a typical comment but no one could remember what he was supposed to have said.

It had not been a 'good fight' or a fair one; there had only been three of them and five of us. It had not been very good for one of the locals who I later found out had been taken to hospital and it was not a good one for Tim in our group. He turned up for work but kept complaining about a sore face. When I examined him I could see that the side he was getting the pain from protruded less that the other side unlike the bruises many of the rest of us had. Tim had only been with us for a couple of weeks and it was the first time he had left his remote village in Ireland. It took another day to convince him that we had a NHS system and he would not be going into debt by seeing a doctor. When he did finally go to the doctors he was diagnosed with a broken cheek bone.

Occasional fights after drinking sessions have always been with us and always will be. Once they start many people seem to have a tribal instinct to join in and help their companions, whatever the cause of the fight. I doubt if there are any more fights today than there were when I was a youth but they certainly get a lot more publicity. What does seem to have increased is the number of planned, organised fights by groups such as football hooligans and street gangs.

I have always tried to instil in my sons the art of 'fight avoidance'; never to take any heed of any insults a drunk may come up with while taking the sensible precaution of standing side on to avoid a head butt. I can remember once when I was accused of being a bastard among other things. I calmly replied "you must know something about my mother that I don't, tell me more." There was a long silence while he digested what I had said and then his mood changed and he offered to buy me a drink which I declined.

Mixing Drinks/New Drinks

If you cannot remember anything about it, it was not a good night. On the odd occasions when this has happened to me it has either been after mixing drinks or trying a new one. When I have stuck to a beer I am accustomed to drinking I may have been sick a few times but I could always remember the previous night.

I once had a night out in the Philippines where the beer was quite expensive but the local 'cherry' brandy was very cheap which suited a poor cadet's pocket. The following day I was told that it took a long, long time to wake me up and I remembered nothing about the evening after I had started on the local firewater.

The first lodgings I had when I went to University were at Whitley Bay, a holiday resort on the NE coast well away from the campus in the centre of Newcastle. I soon met a few more lads in the same predicament and we decided to start our student life with a good night out. I had been drinking for over seven years and I had heard of the famous Newcastle Brown Ale before, without ever having the chance to try it.

My first pint tasted OK and I had nothing else all night. I drank it the way I was accustomed to drinking mild and bitter and probably consumed the same amount as I would have done with one of the weaker drinks. The effect was not the same! I woke up during the night to go to the toilet. Not only could I not find the toilet I could not even find my way out of my attic room. The only light was from a window in the sloping roof. I hauled myself up and was soon relieving myself in the gutter. The next day I looked up and realised how far up my room was; without a strong grip my first day as a student could easily have been my last.

Advice; take extra care when trying new drinks or mixing them in any way.

Drinking and Driving

I was brought up in an era when this was perfectly acceptable and although it was an offence there were no breathalysers and the test for drunkenness was 'walking a straight line'. Most of the police force in those days were heavy drinkers themselves and members of my family who were in the force then have told me many interesting stories. The local brewery in Bury was the best guarded building in town because there were so many policemen who called in after their shift and sometimes for a break during their shifts. The Chief Constable of Lancashire once drove his car into a shop window in the centre of Manchester when he was drunk, without any repercussions. I can recall some cases myself. I was once in the Irish Club in Earlestown drinking after closing time with some committee members when a policeman arrived. He just wanted to see that 'everything was alright' and had a few free drinks while he was checking.

I was no different than anyone else and, in the 1970's I had an accident after a long session when I never should have been driving. It could have resulted in a serious injury to someone. In those days the ability to drive after drinking was a macho thing that many people boasted about. I was never quite in that category and always drove much more cautiously after a few. The problem is that after a long session confidence often returns which is what happened to me.

Since then social attitudes have changed and so has technology, and drink driving has quite rightly become a taboo which only a few stupid individuals break. Both my sons enjoy a good night on the beer and started drinking at an early age. One had a job as a barman when he was at school which he only packed in just before he reached the legal age limit for drinking of 18. One thing I have never heard of them doing is driving after a good session. Even today, when they are both closer to retiring than starting work, if I know they have a drinking evening planned I always enquire "how are you getting back?" They always have a sensible answer; a taxi or someone drawing the short straw and driving but not drinking.

Since the change in social attitudes and the introduction of the breathalyser as standard police equipment the number of deaths on the roads due to all types of accidents has fallen to about a third of its peak value. During that time the total traffic on the roads has increased by a factor of about three. The drastic fall in drinking and driving is only one of the factors involved and new innovations in car safety features is probably the main reason.

Despite this there are now campaigns for reducing the current alcohol readings for safe driving even lower. Some even call for 'zero tolerance' so that even people on some medicines would be caught out.

This is stupid and impractical and the present balance seems to be about right.

Drinking Spirits

I seldom drank more that the odd tot of two of spirits until I spent one New Year at my brother's in Scotland. There the culture is quite different from in England especially at Hogmanay. I drank whisky for three days; only the odd few were at the pub, most it was in peoples homes were the measures dwarfed those in the pub.

I was never so drunk that I could not recall what had gone on the previous day but I could hardly be described as being sober for three days. On the fourth day I decided that it was time for a break and never had an alcoholic drink all day. During the night I had a strange dream which woke me up. When I woke up the 'dream' continued! The same grotesque hunchbacked dwarf was standing at the far end of the bed. I just looked at it for a while in amazement, closing and shutting my eyes and pinching myself to make sure I was really awake. Then I woke my wife to ask her what she thought of it; but she could not see it. I finally got out of bed and went over for a closer inspection. It just moved around keeping a short distance away until it finally disappeared and I went back to bed.

When I told the locals about that night I was surprised to find out that "none of them were surprised" and many had experienced the same sort of thing. Evidently it is a typical 'withdrawal effect' from drinking a lot of whisky and then suddenly stopping.

I often reflect on that night whenever I read about people having strange experiences, particularly religious ones. There may be many ways to 'confuse the mind' the way mine was tricked that night. I knew that the messages my eyes were passing on to my brain must be false and the logical part of my brain knew that it was just a fascinating illusion.

If any reader ever has a similar experience they should make the most of it and if they want to get back to sleep just go over and 'confront their demon.'

Sad Cases

During my 'darting years' I played for a variety of teams; some of them very serious ones but the only one I stayed with was a 'social team' at one of my local pubs. Although I won some individual titles during those years the only title the team would have won might have been for organising the best social events or consuming the most alcohol.

There was a group of us who were usually in the same round and there was pressure to keep up with whoever was thirstiest that evening when we started on the beer. Often towards the end of an evening there would be some who had not bought as many rounds as the others and there would be rounds of spirits to finish off.

Two of the more affluent members of the group, an architect and a business man, also often drank with clients or colleagues at lunchtime. Both the evening and lunchtime drinking increased for both of them over the years that I saw them regularly. I cautioned both of them to slow down a bit and even suggested that we should cut out the rounds of spirits at the end of an evening.

When the darts team folded I saw them less and less frequently and we finally lost touch. Later I heard that the architect had lost his job and years later I saw him for the last time in a pub. He did not recognise me and did not even recall some of our darting evenings. Eventually he remembered an evening we once had together in London when we were both working there. He was a sad haggard mess.

The business man's life also went downhill. His business failed and his wife divorced him. He finished up living on state befits. He also looked a mess the last time I saw him. Our last 'contact' was not really a contact; he called in when I was out and borrowed £70 from my wife after promising to pay it back the following week. That was several years ago.

Home Brewing

I first tried home brewing while I was at sea. Cadets could only buy soft drinks and I always spent a lot of time trying to beat the system. Officers always bought soft drinks as well as alcoholic ones and I was always looking for an Engineering officer to swap chits for soft drinks for ones with the equivalent value of beer. On one trip we had a deck cargo of ginger roots and I decided to become more independent.

I knew the cargo was a perk of the captains and a local agent, so I had no qualms about pinching some. I always got on well with the catering crew and a cook supplied the yeast and sugar I needed to make a potent ginger beer. It had barely finished fermenting before we were drinking it; it was a bit 'yeasty' but went down well.

Since then, whenever I have been on a tight budget, I turned to home brewing. These periods were mainly when I was a student and when I had a young family who depended on me. After gaining some experience with various types of beer I started on wines. I sometimes used the concentrated grape juice from home brew shops but wherever possible I pressed my own fruit to reduce the cost still further. Some were freely available in the countryside but I would also visit markets just before they started to pack up for the day. They often had fruit which was 'over ripe' and would have to be discarded if it was not sold that day. I once bought 12 lb of Victoria plums for a shilling (5p in current currency) which made some excellent wine.

I once had a large batch of damson wine which I left too long before bottling and it went sour. I knew it had just formed a bit of vinegar and it seemed a pity to throw it away so I tried my hand at distillation. A friend who worked in a laboratory found me an old fractionating column and I soon had a reasonably sophisticated still. The spirit I made was not the best I have ever tasted and I have no idea what the ABV was. My distillation experiments came to an end one night when I went out and left my wife in charge of it. She forgot about it; let it run dry and set fire to the bathroom curtains.

Alcohol in other countries

The USA prohibited the sale, manufacture and transportation of alcohol between 1920 and 1933. Those in favour of the bill which introduced it called it a 'noble experiment' and a victory for public morals and health. It resulted in a boom in home brewing and illegal breweries and stills. It was also a gangster's dream legislation and there was soon a thriving underground industry which they could control and make a lot of money from. They were often aided by officials who were either simply against the ban or corrupt.

There are now no alcohol free states in America but there are still many counties which prohibit the sale of alcohol. This is because when prohibition was finally repealed by the central government they left some discretion to lower tiers of their administration. Many counties opted to stay dry. Today about 10% of the land area of the USA is dry which affects about 18,000,000 people. The rules can vary from county to county but in the most extreme cases stupidity has really been stretched to its limits. In Mississippi almost half the counties are dry and in theory if someone if moving houses from one wet county to another they are not allowed to carry any alcohol with them if they cross a dry county. (I wonder if their SAT-NAVs have route options to avoid dry counties.)

Some countries still have nationwide bans on alcohol; fortunately these are mainly limited to the Middle East. As with so many bans which apply to general populations they do not apply to the ruling elite. The late King Saud of Saudi Arabia was one of the best examples of total hypocrisy. It is well established that he was sometimes drinking a bottle of the best whisky a day.

The King was not alone, and nothing seems to have changed. My only inside information is from a friend who worked in Saudi for several years. He is a telecommunications expert who used to supervise the installation of the latest technology in the palaces and palatial homes of the relatively small number of people who benefit most from the country's incredible revenue from oil. Some of the places he worked on had very impressive wine cellars and stocks of spirits.

One of the quirkiest countries I ever visited was the Maldives. There is total prohibition on alcohol for the citizens of that country and severe penalties for anyone caught breaking the ban. However about 90% of that countries tax revenue is from import duties and tourism related taxes. The tourists are mainly from Europe and very few of them would consider an alcohol free holiday. Once a visitor arrives at a hotel complex, which often covers most of one of the many small islands',a full range of alcoholic drinks can be purchased at restaurants and bars. Most of the staff are locals and they are not even allowed to clear away empty glasses that have had alcoholic drinks in them so the hotels have to employ ex-pat staff to move and sell alcohol.

Tobacco

Tobacco has a long history of being used for spiritual and medicinal purposes as well as a relaxing drug in both North and South America where the tobacco plant grows wild. They either smoked it in a pipe or just rolled a single leaf to make a cigar.

The first Europeans to try tobacco were the crew of the Spanish ship the Santa Maria during Christopher Columbus's famous voyage of discovery in 1492. It soon became one of the primary products fuelling colonisation. The British helped to spread the plants around the world and it became the main cash crop in what used to be Rhodesia. In the Ottoman Empire it was initially used as a medicine.

Cigarettes only became widely used in the early 1900's. The name is derived from a French word meaning small cigar. Cigarette smoking has therefore had a much shorter history than smoking either cigars or pipe tobacco.

As cigarette sales grew the tobacco companies manufacturing them started to process the tobacco with more and more additives. These included propylene glycol to keep them moist and chemicals to prevent them going out too easily. Ammonia was added to help convert nicotine compounds into free nicotine molecules to enhance the effect of the nicotine. Many different chemicals were added just to give brands a distinctive taste. By 1994 the five major American Cigarette companies were using 599 additives between them. None of them ever listed any of the added ingredients on the packets except for, occasionally, a flavouring, such as menthol.

The number of people smoking in the UK peaked just after the Second World War when over 80% of men smoked and 40% of women. About 15% of the men smoked cigars or pipes, hardly any women smoked anything other than cigarettes. By 2010 the total smoking figures for both sexes had fallen to about 20%.

The main reason for the decline was research that demonstrated conclusively that smoking cigarettes was one of the main causes of lung cancer and many heart problems. During this time more and more research papers were published highlighting the health problems caused by cigarette smoking. The tobacco companies spent millions sponsoring their own research which could usually be summarised as 'inconclusive' or 'more research necessary'; anything to maintain the profits necessary to justify the billions they spent on advertising.

The decline accelerated when governments started to accept some of the established facts and started banning advertising and introducing health warnings on packets of any tobacco product. Banning of sponsorship of sporting events followed.

It is interesting that historically the first leader of a major country to be totally against smoking was Adolf Hitler. Without the hindsight of future research papers, he made many of the same points that are used today against smoking. He would like to have banned tobacco completely but, as the only non--smoking member of the Nazi elite even he had to show some caution outside his personal life. Perhaps some of today's intolerant majority should reflect on that one.

Nicotine is one of the most addictive drugs ever used and is hard to give up as many of the people who have managed it will testify. The negative effects of smoking are well known but there are also lots of facts that have been deliberately omitted or misinterpreted and it is time to list some of these.

Additives to Cigarettes

Most of the research establishing the worst effects of cigarette smoking used data from the days when my father smoked Capstan Full Strength and my best friend's father Woodbines. Unlike today's cigarettes they have no tips to filter out some of the tar. Very few people in this country now smoke such strong cigarettes and there are none legally sold in this country.

There has been no significant research to establish if the tobacco or the cocktail of undisclosed ingredients was the prime cause of the health problems.

Different ways to use Tobacco

Cigarettes are still the main way of smoking tobacco and little attention has been given to pipe and cigar smoking. One change I have noticed in recent years is that the number of women smoking cigars has increased. What is certainly a fact is that governments have lumped them all together and treated them in the same way as cigarettes.

In the early 1990's I had a good friend who left Wolverhampton University where we both worked to become a partner in a new Building Services practice. Roger's specialism was energy surveys and the design of energy saving installations. Barry was responsible for mechanical services and Chris for electrical services. They complimented each other very well and the business started to thrive. They soon realised that they all had an important input into any large project and business would suffer badly if anything happened to any of them. Roger was given the task of taking out substantial life insurance policies for all three.

The most significant difference in their lifestyles was in smoking. Chris was on two packets of cigarettes a day; Barry was seldom seen without a pipe in his mouth, although it was not always lit, and Roger did not smoke.

Roger spent a lot of time getting quotes from all the major insurance companies and soon noted a consistent pattern in the quotes. The quotes for Chris were a lot higher than for Barry or himself. He rang up to enquire about this and got the same answer from all the companies he contacted. Chris was classed as a "heavy cigarette smoker" which merited a 50% increase in premium. **There was no increase for pipe smokers and cigar smokers who were treated the same as non-smokers.**

Insurance premiums are not 'picked out of the air' by biased individuals, nor do they 'emerge' from dubious government committees; they are compiled by actuaries. An actuary is a highly skilled professional who assesses risks after lengthy statistical analysis of all available data.

If the government were really interested in peoples health they would be trying to encourage people who either cannot or, despite the risks, do not want to give up smoking cigarettes to change to a pipe or cigars. The most practical way to do this would be by having different rates of tax for different tobacco products.

Secondary Smoking

A lot of the data on this topic goes back to the days when heavy smoking was normal in some offices. Newspaper offices were the worst offenders. Most journalists at that time were heavy cigarette smokers and there were times when there would be many of them crammed into a small room working flat out to meet deadlines and many of them would be chain smoking. The scene has been described to me many times by a good friend who was one of them. The odd individual who was not a smoker would certainly have been exposed to intense secondary smoke.

Now we have reached a ridiculous situation when the most vindictive anti-smoking campaigners are calling for bans in parks and on beaches. The bans that have already become laws are already having negative effects that are never given any publicity. I know commercial drivers who plan their day around smoking breaks and if they get stuck in a traffic jam have the option of leaving their cabs or breaking the law.

Only last week I was driving up the narrow lane I live in when I saw a van parked at the side of the road with the door ajar so that the wind could have blown it fully open at any time so I stopped. The driver soon emerged from the front of the van and held his hand up to apologise. He must have been desperate for the fag he had in his hand.

The increasing number of foreign commercial drivers are not used to our silly rules or, if they are, will spend time looking out for anyone watching them when they should be concentrating fully on their driving. If the government ever introduced a blanket ban on all smoking in any vehicle I would probably be doing the same thing particularly when I was stuck in a traffic jam.

What research has shown is that there are far more of the 'dreaded' carcinogenic chemicals released from a barbecue than there are from smokers standing nearby. I have never seen any data on bonfires or firework displays but I suspect the airborne 'nasties' are often far higher than from any barbecue. I wonder if the extreme anti's worry about this when they take their children to such events?

Positive Effects of Smoking

The pleasant relaxing effect of smoking is the reason most people do it but there are no doubt other benefits which seldom get any publicity.

The intense stimulation of the mind is certainly one of them. I have often wrestled with a difficult design problem when working in a non smoking office and suddenly found a solution while I was enjoying a cigar outside.

My most dramatic experience was when I was lecturing, only a few years after I started smoking and I was still on cigarettes. I was a few days into one of my many attempts to stop altogether. I was sitting alone in my office. There was a knock at the door and three final year honours students came in. They were having difficulties with some of the tutorial problems I had set. (I never had an appointments system – students knew they could seek help whenever they needed it.) The problems they where having was to do with aircraft propulsion.

I took out a blank sheet of paper ready to explain how they should be tackling the first problem. I read through the question again and again and the piece of paper remained as blank as my mind. The pressure started to build up in me and I could sense them all thinking "If he can't do it how the hell does he expect us to?" I don't know how long I was in that state but I finally managed to break it. I took a packet of cigarettes from the top draw in my desk and lit the first one while apologising profusely. I changed the conversation to something trivial until I was half way through my second cigarette. I then picked up a pencil and what had been a blank sheet of paper was soon filling up with diagrams and equations as I went through the salient points necessary to solve each problem. It was a long time before I attempted to stop smoking again.

On page 89 of Susan Greenfield's very readable book 'Brain Story' she talks of smoking aiding concentration and refers to reports showing that **Alzheimer's disease is less common among smokers than non-smokers.** She quickly qualifies her statement by saying "the health risks incurred far outweigh any possible protection from the curse of neurodegeneration."

My wife's elder sister died about a year ago from Alzheimer's disease and I saw the effect it had on her and her family. There were six of us at a restaurant one day and I had just rejoined them after being outside for a smoke. I just listened to the conversation which was all about 'Ginge' and her current state which included many personal details. Throughout the conversation she was just staring blankly into space completely oblivious of what was being said about her. Her devoted husband was the one most affected during the year before she was moved into a hospice. Malcolm had been a very active man all his life but he spent over a year hardly ever leaving the house. His own health suffered and he was going downhill fast as his wife became more and more difficult to care for. Since she died he has managed to slowly recover and the last time I saw him he was talking about a group he had just led on a climb up mount Snowdon.

According to the Alzheimer's Society there are currently 800,000 people with dementia in the UK which seems an incredibly high figure to me. They also state that the proportion doubles for every five year age group and two thirds of people with dementia are women. The higher proportion of women is interesting since they will have spent most of their lives during the time when far fewer women than men smoked. How strong is the connection? Statistics have shown that there is certainly some connection.

Alzheimer's is the worst way I can think of to end a life because of its effect on other people and the pointlessness of just being around without anything further to offer to society. It makes dying from some of the smoking related illnesses seem almost attractive and of course with a sound mind one can make the personal choice of whether to carry on.

I have noticed that there have been many world leaders during the past century who were heavy smokers and lived to ripe old ages. Perhaps many of them held on to their positions long after they should have given way to younger people. What is not in doubt is that they must have had very active minds to stay in power.

When I was very young I suffered badly from asthma and bronchitis and almost died on at least two occasions when pneumonia set in. (My sister, Maureen died from the same thing before I was born.) The medical advice at the time was that I should never do anything too strenuous and there was a list of activities I should avoid. I was not even allowed to go swimming until I was eleven years old. Fortunately I rebelled against both medical advice and my mother's protectionism. Once I was out of the house I did what I wanted to do; I went for long walks and, after teaching myself to swim, I was as strong as anyone in my class by the age of 12 when I went to the grammar school.

The asthma attacks persisted throughout my youth and early manhood usually during the night. There were no inhalers in those days so I just got up to find some fresh air. Sometimes leaning out of a window was sufficient but there were often times when I forced myself to go outside for a walk until the symptoms subsided.

Asthma attacks can be triggered by contact with a variety of substances. I had some tests done and found that I was allergic to a number of them one of the worst offenders being dust from feathers. I never used feather pillows at home and whenever I stay anywhere else they are the first thing I check for in a bedroom. Of course just changing pillows is not always sufficient if there is still dust around from the feather pillows.

I had occasional significant asthma attacks until my mid-thirties when I started smoking but I have never had one since. There is no way I would recommend smoking as a 'cure for asthma' but my case is an interesting one. If my asthma had started after I had started smoking there would be plenty of people saying "serves you right" or "you brought it on yourself".

I hope the above examples are sufficient to demonstrate that smoking can have some positive effects as well as negative ones. I am however very pleased that none of my children or grandchildren smoke. I would never recommend smoking to anyone but I would strongly advise anyone who is addicted to cigarettes to switch to a pipe or cigars.

The smoking ban in clubs & pubs

On 1st July 2007 the UK government introduced the most iniquitous legislation in living memory when they banned smoking in all pubs and clubs. There was no consultations or opinion surveys of the people who regularly used these establishments; people who seldom if ever used them were in the pressure groups that helped to force the government's hand. The legislation included provision for a review after two years when the repercussions would be known; there never was a review.

I am convinced that many of the more intolerant advocates of the ban had a dual agenda which they took care to conceal. The hidden part of their agenda was the closure of as many clubs and pubs as possible – they are also closet alcohol prohibitionists! They have been very successful in both their aims.

The number of clubs and pubs has been in decline throughout my life and in the decade before the ban, pub closures averaged just under 0.6% a year or 300 pubs a year. In the three years after the ban these figures jumped to average of almost 3% a year which is a total of about

1500 pubs a year. There has always been far fewer clubs than pubs but they suffered in the same way.

I am certain that the figures published for the acceleration of the pub closures are gross underestimates but I can find no official surveys to back up my hypothesis. However any reader can reflect on what has occurred in their locality to check that what I have to say makes sense.

To justify my claim it is necessary to define just what is meant by a traditional pub. It is an establishment where anyone can walk into at any time to meet friends or strangers and play traditional pub games such as darts, dominoes, cribbage, bar billiards, pool, one of the many varieties of card games, or just sit at a bar and contribute to the typical banter and gripes of the day.

It is one of the key hubs of the life and soul of any village or locality. Anyone thinking of buying a house in an area new to them is well advised to visit the local pub to find out details that estate agents and solicitors might not know or, worse still, avoid telling a buyer. It is the best way to avoid having 'neighbours from hell' or making a mistake buying a small business. Some friends were once about to buy a general store with local and passing customers. The vendor's reason for selling was because a new by-pass would kill off the passing trade. My friends found out about the by-pass from the local pub; not their solicitor.

Pubs have always sold food but it was food to complement the drinking that they stocked; they were not places one would visit for a full meal. Traditional bar food was limited to crisps, nuts, pies and sandwiches. Increasingly, larger pubs started to provide full meals in one room while maintaining a normal bar in another. They had now effectively become a dual drinking bar/restaurant establishment. Smaller pubs without the space to provide catering facilities stayed as traditional pubs.

When the smoking ban was introduced smokers were a minority of the general population but they were still a majority among the people using real pubs and the bar areas of dual establishments. Many of the minority of non smokers using traditional bars had no problem with smoking.

After the ban, smokers went out less frequently and stopped going out altogether when the weather was not conducive to sitting outside, standing in a doorway or standing/sitting in a shelter. Even the pubs which had suitable land to build a shelter were told "any shelter shall be exposed to the elements on at least three sides to maximise the chances of people using them still getting wet and cold and minimise the effect of any heaters".

Smokers just started to drink more in their own homes where they would not be harassed. They were some of the pubs best customers and without them real pubs started to close and the bar areas of dual establishments were no longer economic so they became restaurants while still retaining the name pub. The latter is my justification for saying that the figure for closures is a gross underestimation and the true figure is probably double those published.

It is not politically correct to credit the ban with all the closures so instead they blame the economic turndown and the price of drink. When I first started drinking beer, was 5 pence a pint in today's currency and the price has been rising steadily ever since, through good years and bad years. There is no doubt that the smoking ban is the main reason for club and pub closures.

In some villages the last pub has closed, forcing smokers and non-smokers to drink elsewhere. This has led to an increase in people prepared to risk drinking and driving in rural areas.

As pubs closed the traditional games associated with them took a hammering. Darts and domino leagues either went out of existence or contracted from two leagues to only one, affecting the social lives of many people.

Consequences of Ending All Prohibitions

Ending bans and prohibitions of all drugs both legal and illegal would seem to be too drastic an action for most people. However giving individuals a freedom of choice where it does not limit the freedom of choice of other individuals is surely a worthwhile aim. It is even more worthwhile when it benefits the majority of people in society. Some of the consequences of the actions I propose are as follows:

The hardest drugs – the chemically synthesised heroin and cocaine are the main drugs in this category. If these were freely available on prescription from medical practices or clinics specialising in treatments, the users could be sure they were getting a pure unadulterated product. The medical staff involved would soon be able to identify an occasional user who might just snort the odd line of cocaine at a party from the serious addict who had real problems.

The occasional user could be warned of the dangers and those with serious problems offered help just as they are now at the Margret Sharp Clinic in London (named after a friend of mine who had a leading role in setting up the clinic.)

The more social drugs – cannabis, ecstasy, natural opium and magic mushrooms could all come under this heading. These could be sold by any retailer with a licence to stock them just as tobacco and alcohol are now. Each packet would have clear instructions on how they should be used without being abused and increasing any health risk. For example ecstasy tablets would warn about taking fluids to avoid dehydration and cannabis would be graded in terms of strength with special warnings for skunk. For the latter a price differential would be applied by different tax rates just as it is with spirits and beer.

The price of drugs – all drugs would be subject to VAT and an additional drug duty which would depend on the drug. The important consideration with the pricing is that the final retail price would be no higher than the current street price. The drug duty would become another of the chancellor's options to balance the budget each year.

The gangs and illegal distributors – these are the people who would be most affected and would soon cease to exist just like they did in America when alcohol prohibition ended. There would no longer be any motive for gang members to get young people hooked on stronger and stronger drugs until they could dominate and control their lives. There would no longer be the incentive for the sickest cases to steal from family, friends or strangers to feed their habit. There would be far fewer cases of old people being beaten senseless while their meagre pensions are stolen.

There will always be some people whose lives will be ruined and shortened from drug abuse but hopefully the numbers will decline with a more open attitude to drugs and no incentive for gangs to coerce more people to become addicted to the hardest drugs.

Drug use in sports – there are two distinct categories of sports stars that have used drugs. There are those that have taken them purely for recreational purposes and those that have taken them to enhance their performances in their sports.

Two of the best know English cricketers, Phil Tufnell and Sir Ian Botham, admit that taking cannabis after a hard day in the field helped them to relax in the evenings. If a team playing them had been asked if they minded them having a joint just before or during a match they would have no doubt replied "of course not and we will even cover the cost!" knowing that their performances would be adversely affected.

Any sports star is a role model whether they like it or not, and anything they do will be scrutinised by the media. There are often less savoury aspects to many sport stars lives than taking social drugs and they should never be penalised for it in a way that prevents them from earning a living.

Performance enhancing drugs are quite another matter and individuals and organisations that are caught out cheating should be severely punished.

Perhaps the most famous individual case was the American runner Florence Griffith, (Flo-Jo). In a very short period of time before the 1988 Seoul Olympic Games she changed from being relatively unknown to become a world beating champion in all her events by phenomenal margins. Her physique also noticeably changed and soon there were rumours of drug use being circulated which she always denied. She promptly retired to enjoy the fortune her fame and exceptional good looks earned her from advertising deals. She died at the age of 38.

The most famous case of organised widespread drug abuse was the old German Democratic Republic athletes. Behind their successes in repeatedly winning more medals in all competitions than countries with much larger populations was a team of state sponsored chemists who developed new drugs to suit different athletes.

Today more and more complex drugs and masking agents are being developed and only the fear of being caught will deter some athletes from taking them.

Modifying the smoking ban – giving the public, owners of cafes and licensees some **freedom of choice** could take us back to where we were before the iniquitous ban. Then there were smoking and none smoking establishments of all kinds and many that had both smoking and non-smoking areas. The streets were much cleaner and no one was inconvenienced by having to pass smokers huddled around doorways.

The rate of pub and club closures would certainly slow right down again and some pubs, particularly in villages, might reopen.

Holland and Germany are two close examples of countries where bans were considered or briefly introduced until it became clear to their governments that their public, who are now mainly none smokers, did not want them. They had polls and surveys to find out what their electorate wanted and decided to give their people a **freedom of choice**. It is just another government lie to suggest that our ban was forced upon us by Europe.

There are still many states in America such as Nevada where smokers are well catered for but our media only ever give publicity to states where there is a ban such as New York, California and Florida.

For establishments that wanted to operate with smoking and non-smoking areas there could be rules to prevent smoke from entering the smoke free area from the smoking area. I have a textbook on the market (Mechanical Services for Buildings by Eastop & Watson – Longman) and I can assure the reader that there are no technical problems in achieving this in most buildings.

There is no doubt that modifying the ban would produce a boost to the economy. Local tradesmen would be involved in fitting ventilation systems in many establishments but most importantly people like me would be free to organise evenings out and spend money in this country. The social life of many people would be improved particularly those living in rural areas.

CRIME & PUNISHMENT

When I was a young lad I scrumped apples and roamed wherever I thought somewhere looked interesting; trespassing and keep out signs were just a warning to be extra vigilant and fences and high walls were just challenging barriers I took great satisfaction in overcoming.

I was with a friend one day when I managed to scale a very high wall surrounding a stately home. Although the wall was at least twice my height the masonry was old and provided ample hand and footholds in one section. When I got to the top I noted that the ground level was much higher than it was on the road side and there were even some old tree branches leaning against the wall. The way out would be a lot easier than the way in. Gordon joined me and we cautiously started to explore. I made my way across an open area while Gordon watched out for trouble. When I was safely under cover he joined me. We carried on exploring with one keeping a look out while the other moved on until we reached the lawns surrounding the stately home. We soon became familiar with the layout and the escape routes.

We had found our own truly magical garden. It was full of trees and bushes we had never seen before and there were fish in the canalised waterways leading to a lake with an island where there was an abundance of water birds some of which were 'firsts' for us.

We regularly returned to our 'special place' without seeing anyone. It was always on a Sunday morning when most of the staff would be elsewhere and we were soon very relaxed during our visits. We went there one day in late winter and after our usual tour around the woods decided to light a fire to warm up a bit. The spot we picked was only a few metres from a magnificent stand of bamboo (the first I had ever seen) which grew taller than the wall we had to scale.

We took care to use only dry sticks and we soon had a crackling good fire which produced very little smoke. We sat therein deep conversation until we suddenly noticed that a spark form the fire had set alight some of wispy bamboo leaves which covered the clearing. We had used them as tinder but carefully cleared a small section to the bare earth before we made the fire. The new fire was heading straight for the bamboo but by the time we jumped up to put it out it had reached the main stand.

There was nothing that a quick swipe of a jacket could easily have put out in the open but we could not reach it as it crept between the thick stems. We desperately looked around for something to carry some water from the lake but it would have been no use without a hose to thread between the bamboo stems. We watched in horror as the fire grew and as soon as the first thin stems took hold the fire shot up like a bonfire that had been doused in petrol. Momentarily we discussed running to the big house to raise the alarm before turning around and legging it as fast as we could.

Months later we returned to inspect the damage we had done. Where all that beautiful bamboo had been was big black patch but fortunately the rest of the wood was untouched; we never went there again.

I could so easily have had an early criminal record as an arsonist. Later in life my record might have increased whilst I was involved in left wing politics and I have been very lucky not to have been charged with drink driving in the days when it was widespread and socially acceptable.

As it is today I only have a few speeding fines, just like the majority of sensible drivers I know. The only crimes committed against me have been minor thefts; I once had a watch stolen while I was at work and a few bits and pieces were stolen from my garage (which the police did manage to recover). My wife once had a car stolen.

Now crime and punishment is a more important issue than it has ever been during my lifetime. It crops up regularly in conversations with friends and acquaintances. Most people know someone personally who has been a victim of a crime of violence. The media thrives on it. In this chapter I will attempt to summarise the present situation and propose changes that would benefit society. Before I start I would like to warn the reader about statistics.

Statistics

Statistics on crime are always difficult for a layman to interpret. One of the main reasons for this is that the basis for the statistics can change whenever those in authority choose to change them. An interesting example was in Manchester after the riots in August 2011. They evidently used home office guidance to record crimes committed during the riots.

This resulted in the official statistics showing that crime had actually decreased in two of the areas most affected by the riots. This 'trick' was achieved by classing multiple looting and destruction of property in a single shop as being a 'single incident'.

Different figures for crime (also unemployment, etc) can be derived from the same data and a discerning reader will already be aware of this and be able to quote their own examples. Sometimes it is better to trust one's own 'gut feelings' rather than accept the figures politicians quote.

Punishment

Any organised society must have a system of punishments that are known to all its members to be able to function. In a small organisation, such as a club, members are given a set of rules and transgression from those rules results in a warning or expulsion depending on the severity of the individual case.

In a society as complex as a country there is no way rules can be devised to cover every conceivable situation and a much wider variety of options must be available as deterrents. These may vary enormously from country to country and a crime in one country may be acceptable behaviour in another. In the UK some of the punishments used are as follows:

A Warning

In common with any society this is a starting point for a minor dispute or offence. Some traffic offences (for example a light not working) or a dispute between neighbours (for example excessive noise) should be and generally are, treated in this way unless the warning is ignored and the offence repeated.

A Fine for minor infringements

Very few drivers who have been around for a long time will not have been punished for speeding. One controversy on this one is the way speed traps and cameras are used as a way of generating income and boosting revenue by situating them along sections of road where responsible drivers might consider it to be perfectly safe to exceed the limit. I was once caught doing 42 mph in a 30 mph zone near a school where there had quite rightly been complaints of speeding when children where around.

However I was caught at 7.00 am on a Sunday morning when there was no one around and there were no parked cars on a wide road and just sufficient traffic for the police to take down details of one driver before catching the next one. Three successive drivers were stopped. This was a very efficient police enterprise for generating revenue whilst doing nothing to catch the minority of drivers who were a threat to the children.

There is normally a fixed fine for the type of offence I have just described. Is this appropriate? A fixed fine may be a substantial proportion of a low paid workers income and hence a significant punishment. To a premiership footballer, a banker or a top lawyer the only punishment is the points on their licence. A fairer way would be to fix the fine as a proportion of the previous year's income from their tax returns.

In 1997 a speed camera was fitted on the A35 at Chideock in Dorset. During the next ten years a total of 24,259 drivers were fined between £40 and £60. It was later discovered that all the tickets issued during this period were invalid because the wrong name for the road where the offences took place was on the paperwork and all the money was refunded.

There was no mention of how many people lost their licences and possibly their jobs by going over the 'point count' limit.

Cricket star Andrew Flintoff was once caught speeding at well over the limit. He got off when his 'smart' lawyer found that notification of his offence arrived just one day late.

These are examples of clear 'guilt' without any punishment because of legal paperwork. Legal paperwork should never be given precedence over justice and common sense.

A Fine for crimes

A fine is often part of the punishment for criminal offences, usually part of a package including, for example, a suspended prison sentence. As with minor offences any fine should always be related to an individual's income and assets. For example consider two similar cases of shoplifting. The first is committed by someone living on a very low income; a nominal fine might be all that they could afford to pay and all that the justice system would have any hope of collecting. The second clearly has income or assets which make them millionaires and a nominal fine would be meaningless to them.

For such cases a five or even six figure fine would be appropriate. In such cases the defendant is usually represented by a highly paid legal team who if they cannot find a reason to get them acquitted, will offer a offer a plethora of 'mitigating circumstances', often including a 'mental problem'. Tough! If they can afford expensive lawyers they can afford a hefty fine which should help them to get over their problems and our problems of financing the legal system.

I had only just finished writing the above when I read about the case of two footballers, Lee Cattermole and Nicklaus Bendtner. They were both playing in the first team for Premiership side Sunderland and accused of vandalising parked cars near the ground of a local rival team, Newcastle United. What appalled me about this report is that their maximum punishment could be three months in prison and a fine of £2,500.

As first offenders a prison sentence is very unlikely and would not be appropriate but what about the fine? If they are found guilty they should be made to pay all the expense of repairing the cars and a suitable fine. The judge should not have any restriction in fixing a fine.

An astute judge could ask them what car/s they currently owned, (having already done a check on this). The value of the cars they owned or leased would then be a fitting punishment for individuals who are privileged enough to earn a living playing a game that other young people pay to play each week.

Community Service Orders

These are a relatively recent development in our legal system and should be welcomed. They offer the offender a chance to put something back into the community and to develop a work ethic which should make them more employable in the future. Organising such work is a very demanding job requiring a strong character that is sympathetic to the scheme and a good judge of people. An informal chat during a coffee break when people are relatively relaxed can often be far more productive than a 'one to one' ordeal across a desk.

Some examples of work carried out as part of a Community Service/Unpaid Work Order include:

- Environmental improvements such as picking up litter and removing graffiti from walls.
- Gardening
- Painting and decorating
- Refurbishing buildings
- Assistance and support for the elderly or disabled

The only problem with this type of punishment is what to do about individuals unwilling to undertake such work. Reluctance to work can take many forms from simply not attending without a good reason and repeated lateness to refusal to carry out some of the more menial tasks which would normally be a starting point for a course.

Where a suspended custodial sentence was part of the court edict due warnings should be given and, if ignored, the custodial sentence must be applied. If there was no suspended custodial sentence then the case should go back to the court to get one.

Anti Social Behaviour Orders

Anti-social behaviour orders (ASBOs) were introduced in 1998. Magistrates' Courts and County Courts were empowered to make an ASBO against any person aged 10 or older.

An ASBO does not itself give the defendant a criminal record, but contains conditions prohibiting the offender from specific anti-social acts or entering into defined areas. It is effective for a minimum of two years. Breach of an ASBO is, however, a criminal offence.

Although an ASBO can be taken out against adults they seem to have been mainly used for young people. Unfortunately far too many young people seem to regard them as 'Badges of honour' and a status symbol among their friends. This is a ridiculous state of affairs which should not be allowed; learning that authority can be ignored and flaunted at an early age is a recipe for a future life of crime. A custodial sentence in an appropriate institution is the only practical deterrent; otherwise the whole concept might as well be scrapped.

Custodial Sentences

This is the only form of punishment left when the crime is too serious for any alternative or where one of the alternatives has been tried and failed.

An obvious starting point for this section is to ask the question "what is society trying to achieve by sending people to prison?" I suggest the following answers:

(1)   Secure corrective training which will give the individual time to understand what they have done wrong and to prepare them for living a more worthwhile life when they are released.

(2)   As a punishment and deterrent.

(3)   To carry out the above at a minimum cost to society.

In pursuit of the above aims a variety of prisons are available. The type of prison offenders are sent to depends on their crime and the length of their sentence. The likelihood of them trying to escape and the risk they pose to the public are paramount. There are a range of prisons available and the two extremes are as follows.

Open prisons

The definition of an open prison is one which has no secure perimeter. They are therefore only suitable for prisoners that are not considered to pose any threat to the community and are unlikely to escape.

The punishment is the criminal record and the restrictions on personal liberty. The aim of such institutions is corrective training and there are likely to be specific courses available to make offenders more employable when they leave. Education classes are the norm particularly for the illiterate and many open prisons will offer a variety of skills training.

One criticism of such institutions is that some of the facilities offered are superior to those that many honest working people can afford such as Sky-sport television. Where this is the case I would suggest that they should be earned and not automatic. One way is to make them available only to inmates who had completed a proportion of their sentence without any problems.

Open prisons have varying degrees of 'openness'. The ultimate degree of openness is where inmates carry out a full time job outside the prison. (In such cases the inmate should contribute a high percentage of their income to pay for some of the cost of running the prison.) At the other extreme they may not be allowed outside the gates unless they have a special dispensation.

This raises an interesting dilemma for the prison authorities – where are all the inmates at a particular time? Clocking in and out at the main gate like many people do at work or even visiting a gym is not satisfactory; with no secure perimeter there will be other ways of leaving apart from at the main gate. We now have the technology to tag them all so that their whereabouts are known at any time of the day or night.

Closed prisons

The definition of a closed prison is one with a secure perimeter; normally a wall or fence which is high enough to be challenging to cross even with sophisticated equipment – the type of obstacle we are all familiar with from the many films where prisons are involved.

These are categorised as A, B and C with type A being the most secure and are therefore used for the most dangerous criminals.

Numbers & Costs

In 1993 the UK prison population was 44,000. At the time of writing this the number has doubled. Whenever the prison population is discussed the cost to society is inevitably an integral part of the discussion. Historically the UK once had a very low prison population; basically they were just holding pens for people awaiting a trial. The options available to judges at a trial were also very simple and low cost; acquittal, the stocks, the death penalty and deportation to the colonies. All these options were abolished a long time ago except for the death penalty which was removed more recently and I can still remember well. Now is the time to think of new ways to dispense justice at a minimum cost to society.

For serious crimes that result in a custodial sentence or even a community service order a **'prison cost fine'** should also be part of the punishment. For someone with neither income nor assets this should be a nominal £1 but for all other offenders this should scaled up depending on their means. This is an extra cost I am proposing which would be in addition to any legal costs or monies awarded to people they have offended against.

Before looking any further at typical cases it is necessary to know what the costs are. Ken Clarke, the Lord Chancellor and Secretary of State for Justice at the time of writing recently said that it costs £38,000 a year to send someone to prison, (more than the cost of sending someone to his old school – Eton). Others have quoted even more but a rounded figure of £40,000 is a good one to bear in mind. It is an average figure with the category A closed prisons costing a lot more than an open prison.

Some of the changes I propose are best illustrated by some specific examples.

The Lords and MPs fraud cases.

Lord Taylor of Warwick, a former barrister, became the first black Tory peer in 1996 and was jailed for 12 months in May 2011 for fraudulently claiming more than £11,000 in taxpayer's money. He told the House of Lords members' expenses office that his main residence was in Oxford and gave an address he had only visited twice; he actually lived in North London but claimed travelling expenses from Oxford and the cost of overnight stays in London.

Lord Hanningfield, from West Hanningfield in Essex, was jailed for 9 months in July 2011 for fraudulently claiming more than £13,000 in taxpayer's money. His fraud was claiming expenses when he was not even in London; on one occasion he was on a flight to India which was easy to check up on.

Both lords were released from jail in September 2011 after serving about one quarter of their sentences.

At the same time there were many members of the House of Commons who were found guilty of the same type of crime which resulted in jail sentences. These included the following:

Elliot Morley, a former Labour environment minister was sentenced to 16 months in jail for dishonestly claiming more than £30,000 in parliamentary expenses.

David Chaytor was the first MP jailed over the parliamentary expenses scandal and was **released** from prison after serving just a quarter of his 18-month sentence. Jim Devine a former Labour MP **jailed** for 16 months for expenses fraud was released after serving a quarter of his sentence. Eric Illsley, the former Labour MP for Barnsley Central served four months of a one year sentence.

A common feature of these sentences is that the time actually spent in jail was a small proportion of the full sentence. Another is that their 'freedom was limited' until the end of their sentences; the scheme is termed a 'home detention curfew'. There is no need to go into the details of what this involves but it does not sound like it is any worse a punishment than that suffered by millions of smokers; innocent of any crime but with very limited social lives particularly in winter.

A final common feature is that they all had assets and some of them had incomes from outside parliament. They could clearly have been able to pay a significant **'prison cost fine'**. This should have been sufficient to cover the cost of the full sentence they were given in open prisons without any refund for the early release as a minimum. There is no doubt that some of them could have afforded to pay a lot more and should have been made to do so.

Capital punishment

For many years capital punishment in this country had been by hanging and the last execution took place in 1964. However it was only abolished for murder in the UK in 1969 and in Northern Ireland in 1973.

The death penalty remained on the statute book for certain other offences such as enemy spies on naval ships or bases for many years after. For treason it would still, according to the law, have been by beheading.

An amendment to the Crime and Disorder Act of 1998 proposed by Lord Archer of Sandwell abolished these anomalies.

No government has ever tested public opinion on the death penalty but many polls have indicated that most people would be in favor of bringing it back for some crimes.

I have been against a compulsory death sentence for the simple reason that I do not trust our legal system to always deliver a correct and just verdict. I remember two cases very well to demonstrate this.

In 1950 Timothy John Evans was convicted and hanged for the murder of his wife and daughter at their rented accommodation in Notting Hill in London. During his trial he accused a neighbour, John Christie, of being responsible. Christie was a much more eloquent man than Evans and the jury believed what he said.

Three years after Evans was hanged, Christie was found to be a serial killer who had murdered a number of women at his property, including his wife. At his trial Christie admitted that Beryl Evans and her child were among his victims. Sixteen years later Evans was given a posthumous pardon.

In 1953 Derek Bentley was hanged for the murder of a policeman. Bentley and a young accomplice, Christopher Craig were being pursued by a policeman after a robbery. As the first policeman was closing in on them Bentley turned round to Craig and said **"let him have it"**. Craig then shot and wounded the policeman who later died.

At the trial, Crown prosecutors suggested that Bentley meant "Go ahead and shoot him," whilst the defence lawyers argued that he literally meant "Give him the gun" (and surrender). Craig was under 18 at the time which was below the age limit for the death penalty and he served 10 years in jail.

The multiple meanings of so many words and expressions in the English language make it ideal for crossword solvers but in this case it may have cost a man his life.

Whenever I express my views to anyone who supports bringing back the death penalty they will often say "Tough, so what, no system is perfect and there are bound to be a few mistakes." My concern is that it may not be just a few. The media now have so much power to influence public opinion that the police are pressurised to find a culprit and find one quickly, particularly for crimes involving the death of a child or a woman. This is a recipe for a miscarriage of justice. I have nothing against the death penalty for a limited number of crimes in principle but how it might be practiced is another matter.

Those who support bringing back the death penalty to the courts should have no problems in supporting my following suggestion.

Voluntary euthanasia for convicts.

I will start this section with a well known case which only the most extreme 'sanctity of life fanatics' would argue strongly against.

In 1966 Ian Brady was convicted of killing young children who attended the school where he worked and was sentenced to life imprisonment. For once life did mean life and he will never be released.

At his trial the judge described him as "Wicked beyond belief, with no reasonable chance of reform".

It has always been necessary to keep him away from other prisoners since they feel as disgusted with what he did as the general public and would like to administer their own form of justice if they got the chance. Such tight security is very costly and Brady has been one of the most expensive prisoners we have ever had since he spent his first day in jail; however it gets much worse.

After saying he wanted to die and attempting suicide, he went on hunger strike and was transferred to Ashworth hospital in Merseyside where he could be force fed. His costs escalated as be became a burden on the Mersey Care NHS Trust as well as the prison service who still needed to guard him twenty four hours a day.

He has been in Ashworth for the past ten years and I have seen estimates of more than ten million pounds for the cost of keeping him there. The cost of previously keeping him in various jails must be added on to the total cost of keeping him alive. With NHS costs being cut some innocent people will die for lack of funding, can the 'sanctity of life fanatics' justify this?

The types of arguments they use are 'only God should end a life' and 'he should be made to suffer for his sins'; views which make me feel sad and sick. I am sure that the majority of people would have wanted him to die at the first opportunity.

The case of Ian Brady might be an extreme example but there have been many others and there will be many more where a convict wants to die. Anyone who the court recommends 'should never be released' or are given lengthy sentences which make it probable that they will die in jail should be given the choice of ending their life whenever they choose to. I suspect that there are quite a few who have been convicted of the most heinous of crimes and would otherwise be likely to spend most of their time in solitary confinement who would opt for this choice.

Anyone opting for voluntary euthanasia should also be given a choice of methods. It may be an overdose of their favourite drugs, or with a cyanide pill. The more dramatic may prefer hanging in which case a 'hang yourself' scaffold which only required a button to be pressed or a lever to be pulled could be erected in their cell. Whatever their choice, once arrangements had been put in place they should be left on their own for a sufficient length of time to ensure that they were dead. No one should have to observe them dying – the cell window should be shut as well as the door.

All the media should be told is that the prisoner had opted for voluntary euthanasia and was now dead. There is no doubt that they will find a way to get some of the gory details or speculate on them. This is the world we live in.

There are some specific crimes I would now like to comment on.

Theft of metal for scrap

The value of scrap metal has varied over the years more than most commodities. The industrialisation of Asian countries in general, and India and China, in particular has caused a steep rise in prices.

In the UK we reached a point where the scrap value of 'copper coins' was higher than their face value as a currency. One of my local papers reported on the thefts of supermarket trolleys for their scrap metal values.

In 2010 it has been estimated that cable thefts caused 16,000 hours of delays and cost the economy over £1 billion. By 2011 the government were 'considering' changes to the Scrap Metal Dealers Act of 1964 when quite different conditions prevailed.

The Lincolnshire village of Burton Waters lost its electricity supply for the second time in less than a year when thieves stole more than a mile of overhead power cables in October 2011. The cables were crossing open countryside and the culprits managed to get away in the resulting confusion. If they are ever caught they should be charged with the total cost of the disruption which might be more than the money involved in many bank robberies and they should be treated in a similar way to bank robbers.

The metal theft which poses the greatest threat to the general public is the removal of drain covers from the side of roads. Anyone caught should not only be charged with metal theft but with deliberately endangering the life of the public and carry a mandatory prison sentence.

Heritage sites are amongst the target for metal thieves. In March 2112 the Daily Telegraph reported on a study which showed that there had been 75,000 "heritage crimes" in 2011. These included other crimes such as vandalism but the most important ones were metal thefts. The theft of metal from church roofs has been around for a long time but has now escalated. There are other thefts which I have never heard of before until recently.

One is steeling bronze plaques from war memorials. Often when I am walking through a village for the first time I will stop and study the war memorial. I note the number of names and how many have the same surname and were probably related. There are always far more names from the First World War than the second which remind me of how stupid and pointless it was. I scan the village and wonder what the population would have been when these, mainly young, men died. The thought of anyone desecrating such a place makes me feel sick.

One of the most spectacular thefts was from Dulwich Park in London. It was a sculpture by Dame Barbara Hepworth which had cost taxpayers £500,000. Having seen a picture of it I wonder about value for money and I am sure that the cost may concern many readers who have also seen it. The value of it may be debateable but the cost is not and if the criminals are ever brought to justice they should be charged with stealing £500,000 and not the cost of the scrap metal.

As the reader may have gathered from other chapters I am no great lover of churches but I do appreciate their architecture and heritage value and it is sad that they now have to spend so much money on security and repairing damage.

It would take a full book to comment on every crime, and someone else to write it; now it is appropriate for me to finish off looking at some of the consequences of the changes I have proposed.

Carrots & Sticks

I believe that there are already sufficient carrots in place to give most criminals the chance to mend their ways and lead useful satisfying lives. However there are clearly insufficient sticks to act as a deterrent.

In the August 2011 riots three quarters of the people arrested for rioting had previous criminal records and almost half of them had committed an average of 15 offences without ever having been given a custodial sentence. The media gave more publicity to some of the minority who had been involved in crime for the first time.

The trend of repeat offenders never going to jail was established long before the riots. Ken Clark bluntly put it down to money. His concern is a real one which needs addressing but the cost of not putting people in custody also needs to be taken into account. Once people realise that they can 'get away with it' there is no real deterrent. **The warnings and community service orders should be tried first but, when they have failed, the punishments should escalate.** Police records should always be available to magistrates, judges and juries before they make any decisions.

Some of the changes I have proposed earlier in this chapter together with a change in attitude by the legal system would in the short term increase the prison population but that would only be temporary until the criminals realised the consequences of their actions.

Judges & Lawyers

Our legal system covers far more than crime and punishment hence I have devoted a separate chapter to it. I remember when I once met a young lady who introduced herself as a criminal lawyer and another member of the group I was with interjected "I thought all lawyers were criminals". He was a policeman who had had dealings with them and I have heard the same expression used many times since then.

The fees that the top ones earn are ridiculously high but not criminal; however the way that they manage to keep cases going, often over many years, to increase those fees many would consider to be a crime. Paying lawyers appropriate remuneration for the work they do compared with people in other demanding professions would save society a lot of money.

Outsourcing Prisons

Outsourcing has been with us for many years now and has grown to the point where it is unusual to hear an English accent for many of the services we use. It has been the growth industry in the last decade and there are now very few major companies who do not use it. Their motive is to reduce costs.

As I observed the industry growing I wondered about which organisation would be the next to adopt it. Then I thought about the prison service and how outsourcing could be used to reduce its costs. I developed my ideas many years ago and have 'bounced them off' many people and noted their arguments against them. The only consistent argument against it is that no government would have to guts to do it.

The government has now come up with a scheme to reduce costs by privatising some of the prison service. This is just a short term fix which is typical of minds which work on five year cycles. Their plan is to find private capital to build and run new prisons. This will save the exchequer money now and burden our children and grandchildren with yet more debt as the private companies recoup profits in later years to justify their expenditure now.

My proposal is much more radical and would save some money now, and a lot more long-term. Tenders should be sent out **worldwide** for setting up and running the most expensive category of jails which currently accommodate our most dangerous criminals.

India and China would no doubt put in a quote but there are many other countries which may be interested. The successful tender would no doubt be for setting up the jail in a non-industrial area where building and labour costs are low. This may well be in a remote site which would increase security and decrease the risk of escapes. Some countries may already have sites which might have existing buildings that could be adapted such as redundant army bases. This would speed up the process of establishing the first one.

Basic standards for the treatment of prisoners would be laid down in contracts and personnel from the British prison service seconded to ensure that they are carried out just as they are now with outsourced contracts in many other industries. The standards need not be as high as the norm in British jails. For example there might be radio but no television.

Prison visits from either family or friends would be a major issue in outsourcing. I would be quite hard on this one. It should not be forbidden but it should not cost the taxpayer a single penny. This would result in very few visits and none at all for the majority of inmates. The prisoners would not like it nor would their families. (They could still stay in touch by post). However there might be a positive side to this for the families. Many criminals may still exert strong pressures on their families from inside jail and dominate their lives. An enforced break could free them from these pressures and make it easier for them to get on with their own lives. A benefit to society is that gang leaders would find it much more difficult to carry on organising crime whilst inside.

For a minority of prisoners 'who should never be released' a transfer to an outsourced jail would be a one way ticket. For others there must always be a way out. A prisoner who had served say five years abroad could be transferred back to a UK secure prison and, in time, down the line to lower category institutions before being released.

Reduction in Sentences

'Time off for good behaviour' is well established but can be controversial in some cases. It often seems to be used to control numbers in jail. One of the few instances I can recall when it was repeatedly turned down was for an inmate who had 'failed to show repentance for his crimes'. At each hearing he gave his reason for lack of compliance with this requirement. He always maintained that he was innocent and could not repent for something he had not done. He is one of the few people who finished up serving his full sentence despite being an ideal prisoner during his time in jail.

I believe that a drastic rethink of the wording of the requirements for parole are needed to cover this situation. I have often asked myself and I now ask the reader to consider what they would do if they were innocent of the crime they were charged with; take a principled stand as this man did or opt for freedom by taking legal advice and lying?

On balance I think that 'time off for good behaviour' is sensible but may be a bit overdone in absolute terms when the general public have come to regard any sentence with scepticism. Despite this I am going to propose three new reasons for reducing sentences.

Voluntary Sterilisation

In my most controversial chapter on eugenics the 'genes or background' issue is covered in some detail. It is irrelevant to what I am about to propose because what we do know is that any child of a criminal is a high risk case for also becoming a criminal. We now have families with several generations of criminal history. I am sure most readers would agree that criminals are not ideal people to raise children. Any criminal sentenced to say five years or longer should be able to apply for reduction in time spent in jail after voluntary sterilisation.

I wrote the above before watching the excellent BBC documentary on Glen Parva in Leicester which was for young offenders between the ages of 18 and 22. It was on 27/3/2013 at 9.00 pm and traced the lives of some of the young offenders and their attitudes to parenthood and the children as well as the spouses of those involved.

What struck me most – and it was repeated in the documentary – "They are **five** times more likely to be to be fathers than other men 18-22 in the same age group outside jail."

Clearly my estimation of five years in jail was hopelessly wrong and it should be applied immediately to those who have fathered one child.

One had fathered a child by more than one mother. Another had been in and out of jail for the previous four years. Some had taken a reasonable assumption that a jail was not a suitable environment for a child and did not want to see them – until he could be released and become a 'proper dad'.

A lot of people accept that one child is enough for them. If the inmates are serious about accepting parental responsibility they should take it now and limit their responsibility to one child. They will expect to find difficulty in finding a job when they come out and this should not be compounded by having another child. (This leads to dependency on the welfare state which concerns us all.)

Sterilisation is now widely accepted as the ultimate method of birth control and I know many people who have undertaken it. I took this option over thirty years ago and have no regrets. Encouraging criminals to do the same is hardly a drastic 'infringement of their human rights'.

Voluntary Castration

This is probably a more controversial proposal and very sexist since it would only apply to men whilst voluntary sterilisation would not.

My target is serial sex offenders particularly those who have attacked children. Some of these people should never be allowed out unless means can be found to ensure that they do not reoffend. It is used in some other countries, including Germany. It is contentious there and has been described as 'mutilation' and 'degrading' in various reports against it. The terms used in these reports are more appropriate to describe the way the criminals treated their victims. I think we should try it out in the UK.

Voluntary Drug Testing

Clinical trials always need to be carried out before any drug is available to the general public. In the past many notable researchers have used themselves as guinea pigs; nowadays we use volunteers from the general public. There are advantages in using inmates for tests, such as close control of diet, lifestyle and exercise. Taking part in such tests would enable prisoners to put something positive back into society which would justify reducing their sentences.

Summary

Some of the changes I have proposed are 'stand alone' changes; others are linked and some only require a change in attitude to interpreting existing legislation. If most of my proposals were ever adopted I am sure that the prison population would fall and we could be discussing closures, instead of building more in the UK.

Finally the cost to the taxpayer would be drastically reduced which would please Ken Clark. It would also please most of the rest of us who are taxpayers.

THE LEGAL SYSTEM

Imagine – we all wake up one morning and there are no lawyers.

Perhaps a strange selective virus has wiped them all out.

What would we do without them?

For the vast majority of people the immediate impact would be zero. We would still carry on with our lives as normal; go to work, go shopping, read newspapers, watch television and carry on with any planned social activities.

For a small minority there would be serious, immediate repercussions. Consider an extreme case of someone accused of murder, the family and friends of the accused and the family and friends of the deceased; what about them?

If the trial had already started, a jury of laymen would already have been appointed. There would still be clerks to see to the paperwork. The key players missing would be the judge and the lawyers for the defence and the accused.

Just imagine a local magistrate replacing the judge and the trial continuing without any lawyers/barristers (call them what you like, you all know who I am writing about.)

Witnesses, experts and anyone with a contribution to make could still be called from both sides to present all the relevant evidence. Once they had given their evidence they could then be questioned by any member of the other side and any member of the jury. There would be **no barred questions** and **no inadmissible evidence**. The jury would know the history of the defendant, good and bad.

The magistrate would keep order and set time limits on anyone becoming repetitive and starting to waffle (although there are very few people other than lawyers, salesmen and politicians who are capable of doing this.)

Finally the jury of twelve would give a verdict which would need a majority of two. (With anyone undecided allowed to abstain, a 6-4 majority would be sufficient for a guilty verdict but a 6-5 would not and the defendant would be freed.)

With no 'smart' lawyers involved I suspect that the trial would take far less time and be more likely to result in a just verdict.

Any lawyer reading this will be mumbling derogatory adjectives which might be summed up as "what the hell does this arrogant bastard know about the law".

Well - we have all been involved with the law at sometime in our lives and most of the people I have discussed it with have stories of woe and dissatisfaction. To listen to more positive outcomes I would have to meet more of the criminal fraternity or people who have received ridiculous compensation for trivial accidents. However I will offer the lawyers a summary of my own humble encounters before I suggest some modifications to our present system.

Personal experience

I have some limited personal experience of the law and their archaic ways. I once undertook the selling of one property and the buying of another without any legal assistance. It was back in the early seventies when I was very short of cash and the obstacles they raised to stop me could fill enough pages for another book.

The property I was trying to sell was in the middle of a newly built estate. I never used estate agents and the solicitor told me that I would have to go to the local Water Company to check if they had any right to cross my land. I arranged an appointment with the water company and they were at first amazed to see what I had come for. Then I told them why I was there. They started to chuckle and explained that a right of way was a proposal which had been sorted out when the estate had been proposed over ten years ago. They had never seen a solicitor since then. They then provided me with a document to say that I had been there.

It went on and on with this line of questioning from their solicitor. The final example was the refusal to accept a final transfer document without giving any reason – just advice to get legal assistance. I finally nailed that one – the wrong colour of tape binding the document; it was red when it should have been green! By the time we had reached that stage I told the solicitor that I would be contacting his client direct. The client was desperate to move in but there was a hold up on they place I was buying and I said I could wait until his solicitor could accept a different tape from the norm. The solicitor then sent me a tape of the right colour and the transfer went through.

I had the same trouble with the house I was buying. It was a new house again in the middle of an estate which was partly built and partly unfinished. Again I had a series of questions which they never asked of other solicitors. Eventually they decided that I had to come to their office. I came and was amazed to know how little they new about the estate they were selling.

They had never visited the estate which was well over 50 properties. I spent a lot of time explaining the boundaries. For example they wanted to know what was over the boundary wall adjoining the property I was about to purchase. I told them it was an access to some council dwellings of about 2 m wide. No room for a car but ideal as a second access. I had done my home work, well before I started to purchase the property – they had not. When I left they thanked me for explaining the layout and the purchase went through.

One of the things I did was to be aware of the pitfalls before attempting the above. For a seller the main thing is to get the money owed. For a buyer the main thing is to insure the property at the final contract.

I also carried out my own legal work during the divorce from my first wife. There was never any problem with my main concern – access to the children. We came to an amicable arrangement about money, which her lawyer disapproved of since he wanted to boost his fees by taking out a court order against me. This aspect of the divorce rather backfired on me when a year later I realised that money paid out under a court order was tax deductible whereas money paid through an amicable arrangement was not. I soon found myself involved in legal matters again. The solution was very simple – *I took out a court order against myself!* I can still picture the faces on the clerks as I filled in all their forms – it was a first for them as well as for me.

Many years after that, I had problems being granted probate when my father died. He had made out a very simple will leaving all he had to be divided equally between me and my brother. It was a very modest estate and all the legal requirements had been followed when the will was drawn up. Unfortunately the will had been drawn up in England where my father had lived all his life but he died in Scotland while staying with my brother who has lived there for most of his life. The legal system in Scotland is not the same as in England and I was told I needed a solicitor to reconcile the two systems. I knew that the last thing my father would have wanted was to leave money to a solicitor. I eventually found a minor official who was prepared to sign the necessary papers in return for a couple of bottles of the best Scotch whisky. This may not have been strictly legal but it was justice and a victory for common sense – a rare commodity these days.

I know my father would have approved of my actions concerning his will but he has left me with one further problem – how to dispose of his remains. We only ever discussed such matters during a good session on the beer. I knew he had no problems with cremation but there was never a definitive answer as to what should come next. His simplest response would be "the compost heap", a more elaborate one would be to scatter a few ashes in each of the pubs and clubs he had frequented – an impossible task. I am still undecided about that one and his tasteful oak urn is still on the top of the bookcase behind me as I am writing this. I suppose I am passing on the problem to my children for when they decide what to do with me.

The Alternatives

My opening in this chapter was deliberately provocative and yet all I did was investigate a limiting case where society had no lawyers. The other extreme limit would be if we were all lawyers. It is a technique that scientists and engineers use all the time. For example there is an optimum airspeed for an aircraft powered by a propeller, above and below this speed the propulsive efficiency is reduced; very severely if the speed is too high. If this logic is applied to the law perhaps there is an optimum number of lawyers that would provide an ideal service to society and if there are too many they would have a severe negative effect.

Before I make any suggestions I would like the reader to ponder on the following questions:

(1) Do we have an optimum number or lawyers?
(2) Do they serve society well by achieving what people expect of them?
(3) Is their remuneration and cost in keeping with the job they do compared   with people in other professions?

Job Specification

To answer the above questions it is necessary to ask another one. What are lawyers supposed to do, what do we expect of them? Two very simple and general definitions might be:

To uphold the law
To see that justice is carried out.

I am sure that any lawyer would argue that these are the same thing. I am not so sure; far too often I have read about someone or watched them on television who later admits to being guilty (or just knowingly smiles when interviewed later) after escaping justice because of a 'legal technicality' because of 'smart' lawyers for the defence outwitting those of the prosecution lawyers.

A simple example, which I can easily recall without doing any research, involved the England cricket hero Andrew (Freddy) Flintoff. He was in court on a speeding charge – well above the limit. Most people would have simply paid up and resolved not to do it again, or at least to take more care and not be caught again. Freddy hired a 'smart' lawyer who found that the summons had been delivered just 24 hours late and got him off. For Freddy the legal costs were well worth while – not simply to keep the points off his licence but the publicity kept him in the public eye making him a more marketable product for after he retired from cricket and became a full time 'personality'.

A more serious case is the Abu Hamza farce. Even a Judge said it was 'unacceptable' that a case could go on for eight years – and is still going on. He has never contributed a penny to the exchequer despite having hordes of kids which he expects the taxpayer to pay for. He has been fighting extradition to the US where is wanted for terrorist activities. I do not know of anyone who says that they can have him now (apart from lawyers). In the meantime he has produced more children who will one day take up arms against us.

I suspect that these two examples are sufficient to prompt the reader to recall many other cases when the **'law won and justice lost'**.

My answer to my last question is that my primary concern is to see that justice is carried out and I hope that most readers will agree with me.

To many or far too few

I doubt if many readers will have answered the question I proposed above with insufficient lawyers. I would say that they could be cut by half. The reasoning behind this is, the increase in specialisation of lawyers. Part of this is due to the government pushing through legislation which they have not thought through. Part of it is due to interference by the EU. Court cases take far too long to reach a verdict. The top lawyers and barristers can earn over a £1,000,000 a year. This should be halved and so on down the line. Only then would we see a system where they can be paid a reasonable income compared to engineers which we are desperately short of.

If we have flawed laws that often fail to see that justice is done in an economic way it is time to change the laws.

PROSTITUTION

Prostitution has been around ever since mankind started trading between communities which were remote from each other. The people involved in transporting goods spent long periods away from home travelling by land or sea. I spent nearly two years of my life in the merchant navy so I have some experience of the ports around the world.

It is not technically a crime in this country. However there are many criminal laws restricting how it can be carried out which effectively make it a crime. These include soliciting for work, kerb crawling, living off immoral earnings and strange complex laws governing where it may take place. It certainly takes up a lot of court and police time which is costly to society.

Some situations involving prostitutes many readers may recall and are well worth summarising here.

One is the 'Profumo Affair' in 1963. John Profumo was the Secretary of State for War in Harold Macmillan's government at the time. The other key people involved were Lord Astor, an osteopath Dr Stephen Ward, Yevgeni Ivanov (the senior naval attaché at the Soviet Embassy) and two prostitutes Christine Keeler and Mandy Rice-Davies.

The defendant in the court case was Dr Ward who was accused of living off the immoral earning of the two prostitutes (although as a society Doctor he had ample income from more orthodox sources). The case against Ward soon became almost irrelevant compared with some of the revelations uncovered during the evidence which was presented. These centred on parties held at Lord Astor's mansion at Cliveden in Buckinghamshire where Profumo met the prostitutes. It also emerged that Keeler had a relationship with Yevgeni Ivanov during the same period she had a relationship with Profumo. This was at the height of the Cold War and the serious defence implications as well as the scandal are credited with helping to bring down the government.

The case escalated as key figures giving evidence were subsequently shown to be lying on oath. Lord Astor denied having an affair with Mandy Rice-Davis to which she famously replied "'Well, he would, wouldn't he?" This if often misquoted as "Well he would say that, wouldn't he?" and by 1979 this phrase had entered the third edition of the *Oxford Dictionary of Quotations*. This is one quotation where I, in common with the Oxford dictionary and many other people, prefer the modification to the original whenever I use it.

Another interesting revelation involving prostitutes was published by the Sunday Mirror in 2010. Wayne Rooney, the £100,000-a-week Manchester United and England football icon paid for secret hotel sex sessions with £1,000-a-night prostitutes while his wife Coleen was pregnant with their son. Twenty-one year old Jennifer Thompson was one of the ladies named who he saw seven times over a four month period. He met prostitutes at VIP haunts in Manchester such as bars, clubs and a casino. There have been many other cases reported where highly paid sports stars have used the services of high class prostitutes.

Singers and actors have also frequently made the headlines over encounters with prostitutes. One of the most publicized was actor Hugh Grant in 1995. At the time he was 34 and already a star after the successful film 'Four Weddings and a Funeral'. What made this case a bit different is that the lady only charged $50 – hardly a 'high class hooker'. Sixteen years later the press decided to look her up, presumably to 'celebrate Grants 50th birthday!' Divine Brown had been able to retire after making a million from selling her story and was then happily married with three children. Grant of course is still making millions. This was a 'Hollywood happy ending' for everyone.

More recently, in September 2011 it was reported in the press that Paul Hopes, the former head of 'Toys R U s' had spent an incredible amount of money on prostitutes. This was only revealed during a court case which was trying to recover some of the money he had stolen from his company. It was reported that he paid one of the prostitutes, Dawn Dunbar an estimated £1.7 over a number of years.

The reader can no doubt think of many other examples of prostitution in 'high society'. What they all have in common is that neither the prostitutes nor their clients had committed any crime in terms of exchanging money for sex since there is no law against it.

Some of our high class 'escort agencies' are also quite legitimate provided that the organisers do not receive money from any sexual encounters. If they only offer people to keep someone company for an evening and anything else which may take place is strictly between the escort and the client they are not breaking the law. (However it is very difficult to detect any subsequent payment in cash which may follow a sexual encounter.) There are many business people away from home who might simply prefer to pay for some company over a meal without any thought of a sexual encounter which provides an ideal cover for those who want more than just company.

Many people may naively think that prostitution always involves a man paying a woman for sex. This is not the case and many agencies will offer male escorts for women. In cities such as London there are agencies to cover the full spectrum of sexual preferences. The more exclusive and expensive the agency is the less likely it is to advertise its services, this suits the clients who use them.

At the other end of the social spectrum the laws of the land are applied rigorously to both prostitutes and their clients. Prostitutes can be regularly fined for soliciting and often finish up in jail. Clients may be accused of kerb crawling resulting in a fine and publicity which could ruin their lives. The only people often involved in this field of activity who deserve punishment are pimps who take most of the money but are much more difficult to bring to justice.

Prostitution in this country is clearly yet another case of **'one set of rules for the rich and quite another set of rules for the rest'**.

Sexual needs have no class boundaries and it is time for a complete rethink of the way that we deal with them in this country. There are plenty of examples of alternative systems both in Europe and across the world which we can learn from.

The changes I am about to propose would cater for the needs of all classes, drastically reduce sex crimes against innocent women and children and save the country a lot of money by reducing police and court time. There are no drastic changes to the law required; the changes I propose are minor ones, the ramifications are much more substantial. The main change is one of attitude by our rulers who must accept the following:

(1) It is here to stay and no amount of coercion and persecution is going to stop it.
(2) It satisfies a basic human need.
(3) The present system produces and encourages real criminals.
(4) With no controls the present system increases the spread of sexually transmitted diseases.

(5)   With no socially acceptable outlet for their desires there are some people who will suppress their feeling until they reach a breaking point when they attack innocent members of the public.

(6)   The present system costs the country a lot of money.

I propose the following changes which should transform what is now considered a problem into just another industry.

Restricted Red Light Areas

There are already effectively red light areas in many of our large towns and cities. As they are today they certainly are problem areas. This is because they are not defined and restricted but merge with normal residential areas. The resulting clashes result in many of the cases the courts have to deal with. These areas are normally areas of low cost housing and I have friends who have lived in them. They were single at the time and could handle it but it must be a horrendous situation for anyone with a young family.

Once an area has been designated and clearly marked and signposted these conflicts should end. To ensure that they do, the crime of soliciting should be modified to 'soliciting outside a designated area'. If clients and prostitutes have places where they can freely meet it should seldom need to be enforced.

Red light areas can take many different forms and any well travelled reader is likely to have seen some of them.

In countries like Holland where I worked for two years prostitutes often advertise by sitting behind the windows of buildings which face a street. (This is a very sensible arrangement in winter when the temperatures can be much lower than in the UK.) There are two red light areas in The Hague although the one in Amsterdam is the one tourists' are most likely to have seen.

Clubs

As the examples above clearly demonstrate there are high class clubs in the UK which may allow prostitutes to work without any interference from the law. There is nothing to stop anyone joining these although they may need to be proposed by an existing member. In practice the price of the drinks preclude anyone but the very rich from using them. In the UK the only clubs I have an extensive knowledge of are working men's clubs such as the one I lived in for a while during my youth.

However I can well recall a very interesting experience in a very high class club in Rotterdam in the late 1960's. I was quite a junior engineer in a London design office at the time when I was sent to Holland to supervise the installation of refractory linings in high temperature waste heat boilers and transfer lines, for an ammonia plant. Once on site I was no longer in a junior position since I was in sole charge of all the work and answerable only to the site manager and my boss in London. The contractors for the work were Plibrico who provided the materials and labour. They are still a company known worldwide in the insulation field.

Normally such work would be left to the contractors and the companies inspectors on site. However we were using Insulag, then a new type of insulation which gave off hydrogen which built up significant pressures while it was setting. There were other major plants in the pipeline which the contractor wanted after proving them on this job. There were lots of problems which I somehow managed to overcome and I soon realised why I had been sent out.

While I was there my London boss, Arnold came over for a visit to review some future work on the towers and see how I was getting on with the transfer line and boilers. While he was there he confided in me that the head office in America had already decided to use bubbled alumina on future plants so the Insulag era would be a very brief one. (It was much easier to install and would not require specialist supervision.) Of course on no account were Plibrico to get wind of this.

Like many other senior personnel in the petrochemical world Arnold could be quite abrasive in the office but was very sociable once he had had his first couple of drinks in a bar. That basically sets the scene for my memorable night out in Rotterdam.

One night the managing director of Plibrico invited me and Arnold to join him for a 'night on the town'. Arnold had some influence in Kellogg but I was very surprised to be included. We met in a very plush bar; it was the sort of place that I might have gone in once until I realised how much the drinks cost and then made the one drink last until I had filled up with some of the olives and cheese and onion freebies before leaving. Arnold told me to relax, the only money I needed might be for a taxi back to the hotel.

We visited two more similar bars and in each one the Plibrico boss was greeted as the valued customer he clearly was; in the second one that included a kiss from a very attractive barmaid. We had several drinks in each bar before we moved on to the Embassy Club.

We were immediately taken to a table on the second floor which had presumably been pre-booked because it was the optimum viewing point for the stage on the ground floor. The entertainment was nothing that could have offended any typical family audience. The most provocative act was two flamenco dancers. As soon as they had finisher their act they came up to join us as the waiter arrived with a bottle of champagne. I decided I was not going to mix my drinks and ordered another beer.

I was just starting to feel like the proverbial 'spare prick at a wedding' when the Plibrico boss called the waiter over again but this time it was not for more drinks; it was for a lady to join me!

Laila was an incredibly attractive young Dutch lady in her mid twenties who spoke perfect English. The table the others were at would have been a bit crowded for six and we were directed to another table nearby. I felt a bit embarrassed at first but we were soon in deep conversation and there were no taboo subjects.

She worked at the Embassy club during the week but spent most weekends at a second home by the coast. She could make a basic income from her share of the cost of the expensive cocktails she was drinking and never felt compelled to do anything else. She did of course do more but usually only two or three times a week with a small number of regular clients and her price for one night was higher than I was earning in a week. She talked about her clients without mentioning any names except for the Plibrico boss. She was one of three girls at the club who regularly saw the Plibrico boss. She said that he was a sad man who would often pay for a girl for the night and then fall asleep without managing very much.

When Laila asked about me I told her I had a relatively low position with Kellogg and that I was happily married with three young children. Very early on I told her that it might be more profitable to her to move on and talk to someone else. Then I turned the conversation round to socialism and gave reasons why she should change her way of life. There were lots of smiles and laughter and we must have talked for a couple of hours.

It was about 2.00 am in the morning when I made my way to the door to leave. Laila came with me and just as I was about to thank her for a most memorable evening she put her arms around my neck and gave me one incredible kiss that I will never forget. My knees weakened and momentarily so did everything else. When we parted she looked up into my face and said "You are one of the most interesting men I have ever met, I will break a golden rule and you can come to my place and you don't have to worry about any money." It seemed like an eternity before I managed to reply "I'm sure it would be wonderful but you know why I can't." I tore myself away and felt very pious as I started on the long walk back to my hotel.

Laila was a very level headed woman with plans for her future. She was continuing her education during the day with a view to a career change before she reach thirty when she would have made sufficient money to start her own business. In later years when I had lost my youthful idealism and was not in a stable relationship I often fantasised about how that evening might have ended.

I can see no logical reason why clubs can not be established in the UK to cater for the needs of much wider social groups.

City or 'out of town'.

The arguments for and against are similar to those for supermarkets. There are many large properties in the countryside which are currently being revamped as country apartments or left to degenerate. An alternative use for some of them could be sex clubs. Some of the states in the USA have a variety of such places.

Sexually transmitted diseases

Anyone working in the sex trade should be required to carry a card showing when they last had a check up for sexually transmitted diseases and should show it to any prospective client.

This, together with 'protected sex' should make the chances of catching something nasty from a prostitute less likely than a one night stand with a stranger which seems to be becoming more normal among the young people of today.

Age Limits

There must be a lower age limit for anyone working in the sex trade. It may be contentious what this limit should be. It might be sensible to limit it to the age of consent for marriage or the age at which someone in the armed forces can be sent to fight and possibly die for 'Queen and Country'.

To enforce this all sex workers should be made to carry an ID card which should also be shown to any prospective client. In another chapter I make out a case for us all having to carry one but the sex trade is a clear priority.

Social Acceptability

Once everyone knows that there are acceptable outlets for their sexual needs there should be far fewer breakdowns in long term relationships. Sexual needs are invariably a major part of the start of any relationship but after twenty or thirty years in a relationship one of the partners may have quite different needs to the other one. Consider an extreme case where one partner has had an accident which has left them incapable of 'normal' sex and no interest at all in the subject whilst the other partner still has a healthy sexual drive. Over the years they may have brought up a family; developed many common interests, and do not want the relationship to end.

The partner who still has the sexual needs may suppress them for a while until they meet someone else which may result in the end of more than one relationship. It does not take such an extreme case as the example I used for this to happen. Relationships are far more likely to carry on 'until death us do part' if the partner with the sexual needs finds an outlet for them without any emotional involvement. In some cases the non active partner may have no idea what is going on; know but just 'turn a blind eye' and in some cases know about and approve of it, and may even have suggested it.

The other groups of people who could benefit from a more open attitude to sex are those outside relationships, particularly those who have never had one or find it difficult to talk to people they are attracted to. We can include an individual who becomes obsessed with someone who is not interested in them. With no outlet for their frustrations such people may eventually be driven to rape or a sexual attack.

Once when I was on a long term contract in Holland I remember a detailed discussion I had on this subject with a Dutch colleague. At one point in the discussion I asked him how common the crime of rape in the Netherlands was. He thought about it for a long time before replying "Oh it does sometimes happen here Bill". I cannot imagine anyone in the UK today responding in that way to the same question.

'Real Criminals'

The current situation in the UK is responsible for the gross exploitation of prostitutes either by individual pimps or organisations. The former are normally 'home grown' and the latter people from other countries. They both rely on the threat of violence against both the prostitutes and their families to keep them working. They both take most of the money earned, leaving the prostitutes with very little. Occasionally they are exposed by the media and any reader will have heard about cases where young girls are recruited from abroad with the promise of other work and then find themselves prisoners in a quite different industry with no one to turn to.

The majority of clients who use the services of people coerced to work in this way are unlikely to know anything about their background. If they did, and there were alternatives, very few people would have anything to do with them.

Of course people organising any industry will make money from it. Landlords, bar and club owners need to make a profit. The important point is that if prostitutes do not like the terms being offered they should be free to look elsewhere for better terms or take up another occupation.

With a more open attitude to the sex industry the criminals organising it today would soon have to look for other work.

Examples in other countries

Holland is the nearest example to the UK where there are totally different attitudes to the sex industry. I spent almost two years working there and met many people who had used the sex industry regularly at sometime during their lives. I never heard of any cases of gross exploitation or coercion of the people working in the sex industry. On occasions a group of us would finish off an evening on the beer with a stroll through one of the red light districts in The Hague just for a bit of friendly banter and there were always other people around who seemed to be doing the same. It was probably only a minority who were prospective clients.

In Thailand the sex industry recruits many girls from remote 'up country' villages. They know what they are taking on and have decided that it offers a better life than toiling up to twelve hours a day in the paddy fields. They know that they can increase their income by at least a factor of five and a lot more for the most successful ones. In general they hear about it by knowing other girls who have followed the same path.

I have several friends who live there and through them I got to know some of the people who ran bars in Bangkok and Pattaya. When I first went to work there my friend Andy soon recruited me to play for the pool team in his local bar. The girls who worked in the bars were naturally a regular topic of conversation. Whilst most had similar backgrounds they had very varied lifestyles. Some had just one relationship, usually with an expat, and worked in the bar just as a barmaid in the UK would. Others were clearly 'on the game' and could be quite a nuisance at times.

Most of the girls seemed to enjoy their work but there were exceptions. One girl had only just arrived from her village and was clearly out of place; after only one week she left to go back to her village. At the other extreme I heard stories of girls who had managed to make sufficient money to buy land or a business in their villages where they had become part of the local upper class. I noticed others who changed bars while I was there but I never came across any enforced coercion, although no doubt there might have been some.

Revenue

All prostitutes of any gender or sexual preference should be registered with the Inland Revenue so that they can pay their fair share of taxes. Many will declare less than their actual income but of course many farmers, self employed plumbers and hairdressers do the same thing and there are 'lifestyle checks' when a tax inspector suspects a serious underpayment.

I know that there are a few who do this already. Of course they seldom make the nature of their work obvious and transparent. The most amusing one I have come across is the lady who described her work as 'erection demolition'.

Summary

The present system in the UK only works for the very rich. For everyone else it does not. It costs society in many different ways. It could free up the courts and jails and let the police back to beat where they should be. It is time for a change.

IDENTIFICATION (ID) CARDS & DNA BANKS

These are two contentious issues where there are emotive lobbying groups for and against their introduction.

ID Cards

This is hardly a new issue; the only new aspect is the proposal to make them compulsory for everyone.

I once had an ID card when I was at sea – a Merchant Navy ID card. It had a summary of some personal details together with a photograph and finger prints which was all that was practical in those days. It was quite a small card that would fit into any wallet or pocket and I knew that I needed to have it with me whenever I went ashore in a foreign port.

Today anyone who has served in the armed forces will be familiar with them and of course the police have them and should show them to members of the public if requested to do so.

The National Registration Act of 1939 introduced ID cards for everyone in the UK. Everyone included children as well as adults. The cards showed who each individual was and where they lived. As well as being a security measure they were also useful if families became split up after housing was destroyed during bombing raids.

Everyone was expected to carry their ID card with them at all times until they were finally abolished in 1952 after the war ended. In practice many people would have stopped carrying them long before then and I have no recollection of carrying one when I went to school.

In the early nineteen nineties when I was working in the Netherlands I once shared an office with a young German. He was in a bit of a panic when he suddenly remembered that his ID card was due for renewal, and without a current card, he would have to leave the Netherlands. He managed to sort it out in time but never questioned the fact that he needed one. The only thing that surprised him was that we did not have one in the UK. In theory, I was supposed to carry my passport which was not very convenient to carry and I only took it out of the hotel safe when I was told I would need to have it with me for a visit to the dentist or a bank.

On the continent many people will spend part of a typical day in more than one country and having some form of ID is essential at all times.

In this country many people require specific ID cards to go to work. In recent years my first morning at a new company involved a visit to security and I could not even go to the desk I would be working at without being taken there with an existing member of staff until I had one. The swipe card I was issued with included a photograph, taken by security, and I was expected to display it whenever I was on the company property including the grounds. The card only allowed me access to the areas of the building which I would regularly need to use. The only problem I had with this sensible arrangement was deciding whether to hang the card around my neck or clip it to a shirt pocket.

Arguments against ID Cards

Some of the arguments against ID cards include:

(1)   Infringements of personal liberties – the one thing that people putting forward this argument often fail to list are the people whose personal liberties might be infringed.

(2)   We already have too many cards – I agree with this one but most of them just provide people with temptations to fall into debt and pay high interest rates.

(3)   The cost – for many people this might be a burden but if we all had to have one there should be no cost to the individual to get one. The cost should be paid for from general taxation.

Arguments for ID Cards

Some of the arguments for ID cards include:

(1)   Catching 'benefit cheats' – an ID card and cards for any family and children would have to be produced and scrutinised by all claimants. There would be no more claims for bogus families or families residing in other countries. There would be no more multi-claims because once a claimant had registered at one centre it would be put on a national data bank and it would not be possible to make any claims at any other centre.

(2)   Illegal Immigrants – catching illegal immigrants is one of the most obvious benefits of having ID cards. The scale of illegal immigration is now a concern for legal immigrants as well as for people born in the UK.

(3)   Holidays abroad – although 'long haul' holidays are increasing in popularity most of them are to other EU countries where a passport should no longer be necessary.

(4)   Age limited purchases – bar staff at pubs and clubs would be able to ask to see an ID card if they were uncertain about a customers age before serving them with alcohol; the same would apply to staff at shops selling tobacco products.

(5)   Sex workers – having to show an ID card to police or clients would prevent people who were under aged or suffering coercion from being exploited. This topic is covered in more detail in the chapter on prostitution.

(6)   Police work – ID cards would improve the efficiency of many aspects of police work.

(7)   The cost – reducing benefit frauds alone would more than pay for the scheme and produce a big surplus for the exchequer.

Design of cards

There have been a lot of technological developments since the days when I had a merchant navy ID card and there are now several ways to improve on the accuracy and ease of identifying an individual.

The border controls have always had natural concerns over competitors in sporting events just staying on after the event ever since the 2002 Commonwealth games when most of the 30 strong Sierra Leone team disappeared at the end of the games. The ID cards issued for the 2012 Olympic Games included finger prints and face scans. A face scan is not just a photograph; it gives ratios of the lengths between facial features which many experts claim are just as distinctive as fingerprints but much quicker to process.

Another possibility is iris recognition. I am not sufficiently knowledgeable to discuss the merits of the methods available. Any decisions made on the design of ID cards should not be irreversible if another method which is proved to be superior is developed because cards would need to be updated at regular intervals just like passports.

DNA Data Banks

Unlike ID cards DNA data banks are a very recent development and the idea that we should have a national data bank is even more contentious.

There is no need for the layman to understand all the technicalities involved but we should all know sufficient facts to understand how it can be used. A DNA sample can be broken down into different sections just like a tree can be broken down into roots trunk bark and leaves. With trees a sample of one of these parts may be sufficient to quickly determine a general category but a lot more investigation is needed to determine an exact type. (There are over one hundred types of oak tree.)

One of the problems facing genetic scientists is that many of our genes are common to all living creatures and in our nearest 'relatives', the great apes, there is only a 4% difference.

Within this 4% scientists have identified 13 areas of a humane gene which vary from individual to individual. In forensic work a small DNA sample left at a crime scene may be insufficient to identify more than a few of these areas. The more areas that are identified the higher the probability of a match with a suspect. There have been a number of court cases where this probability figure has been contentious.

With voluntary samples all 13 areas can be identified which lifts the probability numbers against mismatches into the realms of the odds against wining the jackpot on a major lottery. There may never be 100% certainty, (there seldom is in any science), but the odds are good enough to make a national data base worthwhile.

Arguments for DNA Data Banks

Some of the arguments for DNA data banks include:

(1) Identifying criminals – this is now widely used in criminal investigations. However samples are only taken from suspects and people the police wish to eliminate from their enquiries. It is not compulsory for the latter although refusal to give a sample would warrant further investigations. This procedure is very time consuming and is unlikely to catch anyone who deliberately targeted a victim from an area well away from where he/she lived. A national data bank would save a lot of time and money and, most importantly, prevent criminals committing further crimes before being caught. Far too often serial offenders may leave a good DNA sample on their first crime scene but are not caught until over a decade later, and even worse are the cases where they never get caught.

(2) Paternity cases – with casual sexual encounters increasing, more and more birth certificates are issued with the term 'father unknown'. In some cases this may be genuine ignorance; in others a deliberate deceit. Whatever the reason, it is fundamental that two people are necessary for any birth and both should be accountable and face up to their responsibility. A search of a local DNA bank would quickly establish who a father was. DNA testing for another category of paternity issues is already well established and may take place years after the child has been born. These are cases where the 'father' on a birth certificate suspects that the child he is rearing is not biologically his own. If this coincides with the break up of a relationship it may not be unreasonable of him to decide that he should have no further financial responsibility for the child. There are now companies on the web offering a DNA service for paternity cases. The advertising blurb on one site claims to offer an affordable price with no frills, bells or whistles!

(3) Identifying accident, war and disaster victims – one thing we can be sure of is that natural and man-made tragedies will continue to take place at regular intervals. Any event involving a fire, explosion or in the worst case scenario both can leave only very small samples of the

bodies of the victims. The longer it takes to identify victims the more heartbreak there is for the family and friends who think that their loved ones may have been involved. The Muslim air attack on the World Trade Centre in September 11, 2001 resulted in the most challenging use of DNA testing. The medical examiner's office received about 20,000 pieces of human remains. Some victims had previously stored medical samples which were relatively easy to match; others did not and it was necessary to take samples from near relatives. Although most of the victims were from the USA many were from other countries and if any of the countries involved had developed a national DNA data bank it would have been much easier to identify their citizens. That may not have been practical then but it is now and we all still live under the threat of future attacks.

(4) Organ donations – accidents which result in a death but leave key organs intact and reusable are a regular occurrence. These present the medical profession with three challenges; limited time before the organs deteriorate, matching an organ to a suitable recipient and getting permission to remove organs. The number of potential donors would be drastically increased if individuals who could not accept the idea of their organs being used to save other peoples lives were required to carry a card clearly stating this. (If we all had ID cards it could be included in the personal information stored in the card.) The matching time would of course be drastically reduced if we had a national DNA bank.

Arguments against DNA Data Banks

Some of the arguments against DNA data banks include:

(1) Infringement of civil rights – this old chestnut crops up all the time. What proponents of this argument seldom do is make out a list of the people whose rights will be infringed. The only people I can think of are criminals who are much more likely to avoid being caught without one.

(2) Misuse of data banks – this is a more subtle argument. It is based on the assumption, not an unreasonable one, that a data bank would somehow be accessed and used by private companies. A DNA profile could certainly be used by insurance companies to assess the premiums they charge individuals. I am not convinced that this would be such a bad thing and paying for access would help to finance the data

bank. Insurance companies currently assess premiums on information we provide such as family history and lifestyle. A DNA profile could add a new dimension to their assessment. This would result in higher premiums for some individuals but lower ones for others.

(3) Cost - there would certainly be a significant cost in setting up a data bank but the long term benefits would make it worthwhile. A bank has already been started by the police and none of the data they collect should ever be destroyed. Anyone who has a medical check up that involves taking samples could cheaply have their DNA profile taken at the same time. It is the sort of project which should not be rushed and could take as long as five years to complete.

Summary

The more extreme members of some civil liberty organisations may well link the two issues raised in this chapter as evidence that I would like to see some sort of police state in the UK. Nothing could be further from the truth.

I know that in any police state people who suggest radically different alternatives to the status quo are quickly suppressed in some way. It is a tribute to the democracy in the UK that I have been allowed to publish this book. No one has anything to fear from my proposals in this chapter and if either were ever introduced the benefits to society would soon become clear.

ECONOMICS

It is Budget time again; and by the time we have worked out the impracticalities and injustices of the old one it is here again.

It keeps happy a multitude of accountants who will be finding ways of not paying some of it and a Revenue staff who don't understand it themselves.

What is needed is a radical rethink of the way we do things. Once we have sorted out what is a just basis of the way we live, we can sort out what we must be doing in the next year. My radical rethink is as follows:

National Living Allowance

The most basic human requirements are water, food and shelter. What are regarded as basic in a developed country are of course much higher than in developing countries. The details of course are very debateable; for example many would regard a television as a basic need, (although I would not), but very few would argue that that the latest model should be included.

It is clear that somehow everyone in our society manages to obtain the 'basics'. Their income may come from working, a pension or from one of the numerous state benefits available.

If everyone needs, and is somehow getting, a basic income then why not simply provide one for everyone? **This should include those working.**

This would eliminate the need for student grants or loans, basic tax allowances, state pensions and, most important of all, our benefits system. This would free hundreds of thousands of civil servants in local and national organisations to be employed in useful creative and productive work.

To consider this topic sensibly I will offer some figures which could apply in 2012: £70 per week at the age of 16, £100 at the age of seventeen and £130 until the age of seventy when it should be increased by £10 and a further £10 added every ten years. I have based the lowest limit on the current school leaving age and the point at which the full allowance is payable at the age which is now regarded as the start of adulthood. The reason for the increases in old age is because people are less likely to be able to work.

Disposable Income

Most of any living allowance will be taken up by essentials such as housing, utility charges and food. What is left over is disposable income where the individual can choose how it is spent. They can save it up to spend on clothes or holidays or spend it weekly on non-essentials such as alcohol.

Where the national income is an individual's only source of funds their disposable income will be very little, probably less than £20 a week. Hardly anyone would want to live on this for any length of time and it should be up to the individual to supplement this income.

The government should provide incentives for people to contribute to sound, flexible, pension schemes. This should take into account life expectancy while they are working. People of all ages and abilities should be encouraged to work.

Minimum Wage and Security of Employment

I have spent a lot of my life as a member of a trade union and a supporter of a minimum wage. However during that time I came across many examples where people who wanted to work were not given the chance because of the regulations in force at the time.

When I worked in the education system one of my jobs was to find industrial training for students on sandwich courses. In the 1970's this was not a problem; most students were already sponsored before they enrolled and the others soon found suitable training placements. By the late 1980's many local engineering companies had closed down and it became very difficult to find training places. I contacted the managing director of a small company to try and find a place for one of my students. He was sympathetic and agreed to help out and even pay the student a basic living allowance. (The student was desperate and would have worked for nothing!) I was feeling very satisfied with a job well done when my contact rang me up to apologise and tell me there would be no training. A union had decided that everyone should be paid a minimum wage and the company could not afford to pay anyone other than fully productive workers.

I have come across many cases right up to the time of writing this when I have met people who would like to employ someone but were reluctant to because of the difficulty of getting rid of them if they took on someone who was not suitable or they ran out of work. One was a vet who was nearing retirement age and clearly very affluent. When I saw him at the pub he would often complain about a new minor injury from a large farm animal (before vets were for pets!). Whenever I suggested that he could well afford an assistant he related one of his stories about someone he had taken on and the problems he had had getting rid of them. More recently it is usually a case of a couple of weeks work 'self employed' or cash in hand which might be repeated at regular intervals.

I have reluctantly moved a full circle on this one and would now propose **no minimum wage** and no disincentives to employing people.

Advantages of a Freer Labour Market

(1) With a totally free market an individual in long term employment which they considered to be satisfactory could still negotiate contracts including clauses such as time limits for terminating employment and ideally, pay increases, related to a company's profits and/or directors' remunerations.

(2) At the other end of the scale it would pay people with only the national living allowance to accept employment for a very low wage. If their disposable income was only £20 a week then working for as little as £40 a week would increase this by 200%.

(3) This could go a long way to solving the current training problems for many young people. In a stagnant/recessive economy many smaller companies can not afford the cost of training new workers. Trainees do not train themselves; they need the guidance of experienced workers. This diverts the experienced worker from productive work. A balance needs to reached to make it worth while employing a trainee. The content of any training scheme should always be approved by a government department and include time to study relevant theory at an educational institution to ensure that any qualification at the end of the training is nationally recognised. Wages paid during training should only be agreed between the trainee and the employer with no government interference. (Remember the trainee will still be getting a national living allowance.)

(4) There are many jobs which are essential for society to function that are not very inspiring and many look down on. However I cannot think of any that offer no challenge at all.

Value Added Tax (VAT)

VAT is a tax which everyone has to pay when they purchase goods. Even a criminal whose main source of income is from theft or dealing in drugs will pay VAT when they buy a new television or car, buy groceries or when they go out to a club or pub. For most people it is much harder to avoid paying than income tax.

Many years ago I had a very interesting conversation with a drinking acquaintance in a pub who suggested that income tax should be abolished and VAT increased to balance the revenue to the exchequer. I immediately recognised that he had done something that I always try and do – investigate one extreme limit of an idea and then look at the consequences. (The other extreme limit of no VAT is something that many readers will remember.)

Stuart had suggested the idea so it was up to me to find faults with it. I did my best but he had the advantage of having given the proposition a lot of thought and had put the idea to other people before he tried me. It was one of those interesting conversations that I will never forget. There is certainly a good case for drastically increasing the proportion of the exchequer's revenue which comes from VAT.

Personal Income Tax

There will still be a need for personal income tax. However for a population which already has the national living allowance it would come into force at a much higher level. I can be graded just as it is now with the wealthier paying more tax.

The unemployed who cannot speak English

In September 2011 the Prime Minister, David Cameron, and the Work and Pensions Secretary Ian Duncan Smith hit the headlines with 'their intention' to target the estimated 70,000 people who could not communicate well enough in English to get a job.

One requirement was that they should take a course in English to continue receiving benefits. All the advantages of such a course to both the students and the general community were eloquently explained.

I am all for such courses which people can and should take up - out of choice – but is coercion likely to work?

There would be Muslim females who might never attend if the lecturer were a male and vice versa; so would it be necessary to provide for two less economic classes? The old adage of taking a horse to water but failing to make it drink would certainly apply to others. Some might just attend without taking anything in; they might even make a serious effort but be incapable of mastering a language which they never use at home or among their friends.

If people choose to come to this country and need to earn a living they should accept that they will need to pass some form of English test appropriate to the job they are applying for. This should mean quite a sophisticated test for professionals such as doctors or engineers but a much simpler test for more mundane jobs.

Without it they would have to rely on the national living allowance if it came into force when they were living in this country. But more recent immigrants should get nothing at all and be dependant on those who brought them in until they find work.

Summary

There should be no set period of work and no retirement. This should be tapered off at the beginning and tapered off at the end until we can die with dignity. The national living allowance should make this feasible for everyone. It is crazy to demand retirement now just because of 'an agreed' retirement date. Everything is controlled by demographics and it is easy to surmise, but difficult to predict, where we will be in twenty years time.

It seems that any retirement is unlikely to be less than sixty five. Before then they should be taking an increasing amount of holiday and then passing on what they know to the next generation. By the time they are seventy they could be just standing in for peak holiday times when those with children will want to take the most time off. Flexibility is what we need.

For the better off who have managed to do well and contributed well above the national living wage in a private pension, there is nothing to stop them going to warmer climates and they can take with them the national living wage which they have earned.

Many will have undergone several changes of lifestyles during their careers. Those who have made their money may want to move on to something new. I can think of many tasks which are physically demanding such as driving a digger or the fire service and they can switch to something less demanding later on in life.

I myself have undergone several career changes. Firstly I have been a Marine Engineer, then a full time Engineer in Petro Chemicals, then an Academic, then a full time Consultant and now an author. I would not rule out any further changes

THE BANKING SYSTEM

In September 2011 I read an interesting article by Edmund Conway in the Daily Telegraph in which he made a very provocative statement that I would have been very proud to have thought of; "why shouldn't banks – at the very least investment banks – be returned to unlimited liability partnerships?"

Historically in the early 1800's banks were unlimited liability partnerships. The partners in banks could make large profits then just as directors of banks do now. The difference then was that if bankers made a series of wrong decisions they could be pursued to repay their debts. Anything they owned, including the mansions they lived in, would be sold off until the debts were repaid.

Quite a contrast to 2009 when some of those who had made the biggest mistakes were handsomely rewarded with incredibly large 'retirement packages' or just shuffled around like a deck of cards to new positions where they could carry on making more ludicrous amounts of money even if they continued to make bad decisions.

Building Societies

Building societies that remained as building societies were untouched during the crisis. They simply organised savings for those wishing to save and then lent them out to people who wanted a loan to buy a house at a slightly higher interest rate.

The difference between the savings and loans was all that was needed to pay the staff and accommodation; they frequently owned the freehold of their Buildings.

In cases where there were more people wanting to withdraw than save, a contingency fund was set up. This allowed a period of readjustment when tougher requirements were made for a loan and vice versa. Typical loans were about 85% and 80% of the buildings' 'worth' at the time of purchase.

Control of Building Societies

Building Societies were extremely local in origin. They were controlled by their members. At an AGM the management had to answer for any adjustment of remuneration from the last AGM. It was not difficult to do this because it only needed a visit down the road to attend an AGM.

No longer Building Societies

The majority, then set out to destroy this image. There were a series of take-overs until they became International Building Societies. I suppose that the 'bigger and better' syndrome took over. They no longer owned their freeholds. Accountability was a thing of the past.

Banks & Limited Liability Companies

Limited Liability meant that they were no longer building societies. They still had AGM's of course but they could never muster enough votes to oppose the management whose demands became greater and greedier.

They decided to do away with the traditional Building Societies' rules of not lending above about 20% of the assets. They were now lending a 100 % of the mortgage some a bit more – to pay for legal costs etc. This justified their economic demands for more and more for the board of trustees.

It had to come to an end.

The housing boom could not last and many people ended up with negative equity. Just as there is a warning that limited liability shares of any kind can go up as well as and down.

I said this at the time – why could not other people understand? It went on longer than I thought, and I was often referred to as old fashioned whose mind was fixed in the past. But my mind was fixed by **history** and the great depressions of the past.

They coined a term "sub term" lending; which covered most of the worst cases. Until then they had been scattered around the banks like confetti. The worse culprit was the US but it did not stop UK banks getting in on the act. More capital and the easier it was to justify bankers' demands.

It came to an abrupt end when some people could not pay their mortgages. The exceptions were there; particularly in Germany and The Netherlands when most people rented property and saved the rest; another was in Canada where their government refused to get on the bandwagon and carried on as they had before.

The latest

The latest government 'initiative" is to try to boost the building economy. As of today, March 2013, they have a whole series or measures. I quote from a government document; "help to buy equity loans", "available for January 2014", "prices less than £600,000", "A Help To Buy mortgage guarantee lets you buy a newly built home or an existing property with a deposit of only 5% of the purchase price", and of course the government will make up the difference.

That of course means you and me and our children and our grandchildren. This smacks as a "sub term" in a different guise and name.

Will they not get it into their thick heads that the housing market has a long way to go **downwards** before it reaches equilibrium?

The building industry can be stimulated by much needed infrastructure. We have talked about the tidal barrage in the Severn estuary since I was a student – do something. We know that there is a problem, (perhaps not this year) with getting water from the North East and Wales to the South East – do something now (the affluent South East can afford to pay for it). Some of the railways which were uneconomical during the Beeching cuts can now be made to pay due to the increase in rail traffic.

Above all the banks should be made to pay; not mortgages for home loans but business loans to help stimulate the economy. (Perhaps government interference could help this time.)

Control of Banks

I for one am finding the banks out of control. Some competition is a good thing for mortgages and my children repeatedly swap theirs to get a better deal. (I stayed with one for twenty five years.)

But saving accounts are a different matter; unless you want to tie up your saving long term. I do not, and have to go through a regular check on who is paying the best rates at the time. Failure to do this will find savings going down to 0.01% interest at the end of the agreed time limit. These should be fixed to no more that about say 70% of the original saving bonds. Or better still an automatic transfer from the old bond to a new one.

Loyalty counts for nothing in this day and age and the banks get a lot of their money in this way. The main people this affects are the elderly and those whose have changed their circumstances due to ill heath and cannot be bothered to keep up with the changes. I regularly hear about the sad story of someone who has been on a 0.01% interest rate for a long time.

Another gripe is banks and building societies being mixed up with travel agencies, insurance etc. If I want a travel agency I should go to one and if I want an insurance company I should go to them. Banks and building societies should be limited to banking and not getting involved with anything else.

Credit Cards

All companies issuing any form of debit or credit card should be legally compelled to display 'financial health warnings' in prominent positions on every page of the card statements. They should also be compelled to show the consequences of being in debt.

Any new form of debit or credit card should be accompanied with a statement of what other cards they currently hold. If one is over the limit and is currently paying ridiculous interest rates they should be refused.

We have to get away from this culture of being permanently in debt. It benefits no one and leads to the least well off in society being lumbered with debts they can no longer repay. I reluctantly now have credit/debit cards, but I also have a standing order that they will be paid up in full at the end of the month.

FOOD and WASTE

About 30% of all the food purchased in shops and restaurants in the UK is discarded. For many years I have been appalled by the 'great Xmas waste'. Just before the big day I often heard people bragging about how big a turkey they had ordered and before New Year they would be talking about how much they had thrown away.

I could not find a single authoritative source for the figure of 30%. However it has been around for a number of years and, since I first came across it, I have watched out for any surveys which resulted in a significantly different value. I have also questioned many people while making my own, very unscientific, survey. I have come to the conclusion that 30% is a very realistic estimate

Some of my solutions would require the relaxing of some of our existing legislation and in other cases introducing new laws. Before I start with some of my solutions there is a recent proposal which shows that some people are making an effort.

A misguided solution

In 2011 some 'not so bright' boffins had discovered that a lot of food was being thrown into general waste bins and generally finished up as landfill unless the increasing flocks of seagulls along with rats and foxes could make a meal of it before it was covered over. They also 'discovered' that food has a calorific value – surprise, surprise, so that the waste food could be burnt in mini power stations where it would produce 'green' energy. The energy used in producing and collecting the 'slop buckets' was not realistically taken into account, nor were the problems of the smells during the summer months and the mess that would result from the foxes learning to open imperfectly sealed buckets.

One basic criticism of this proposal is that it accepts that waste food on the current scale is inevitable and will continue at its present rate. The main challenge should be to drastically reduce it before it gets to any waste bin and there are several ways to do this.

2 for 1, 3 for 2 But None For Others

There are some perishable products which seem always to be on 'special offer'. A single packet may be £1 but two packets are, say, £1.50. It does not require any higher mathematics to work out the 'saving' in buying multi packs.

This gimmick seems to work even with well educated people who might consider them selves to be 'sophisticated shoppers'. It works every time with my wife and often most of the last pack goes off before we can eat it. Fortunately it does not finish up as landfill because we have a compost heap if it is something which the birds will turn their beaks up at.

Apart from the waste it produces, my main concern about this development is the shopper who lives alone, often a pensioner with a very limited budget. They cannot afford more than one pack and realise how they are paying an inflated price for a single one. The most likely outcome is that they do not purchase anything and will be missing out on fruit and vegetables.

The only solution is to bring in a new law to ban the sale of perishable goods in multipacks.

Any retailer knows what average price he needs to sell at to make a profit. It would only take a day or two to change to unit pricing and this would simplify their computer system. They can still increase their prices when supply is limited and reduce it when they need to clear stock.

This simple measure would immediately cut down on waste and improve the diet of those on limited incomes.

Buy One, Get One Free

This gimmick has become so common that the word 'bogof 'has been added to our language. It is widely used for perishable and none perishable goods. When I first encountered it I tried saying "I will just have the free one please". Sometimes I received pained looks from a shop assistant who clearly thought they were dealing with someone who was mentally retarded as they explained that I could only have the 'free' one if I purchased another one. Their expressions soon changed as I started to give a mini lecture on the misuse of language and false advertising. This would normally end as a queue started to build up behind me and I left without buying the controversial item(s).

The only solution is to bring in a new law to ban the use of the word 'free' in advertising when the word is being misused and does not mean free.

I cannot think of any other way to abolish this farce and waste.

Sell By Dates

This is another piece of well intended legislation which leads to a lot of perfectly good food being thrown away. There is no need for legislation on this one; all that is needed is an understanding of the logic behind any dates and some common sense. It is also important to emphasise that the wording is a guarded 'best before' not 'never use after'.

An extreme example of how long food may be stored was some of the grain and seeds found in Egyptian tombs – they were still edible.

Food in metal cans

Some examples of 'best before' dates for food in metal cans are as follows:

Sardines in olive oil – 5 years
Tomatoes/peas – 21 months

It is easy to see why the discrepancies of these commodities. Oil is a preservative and should outlast the other two. As far as sell by dates are concerned just open the can and look at them. A tin containing olive oil will last a lot longer than five years. The other two could be opened and just inspect the damage, if any, between the can wall and the outside.

Food sealed in plastic

Cheese and pate are often classed together as having a quite short life. Pate may be a bit dodgy and I would keep to the recommendations, give or take a few days. Cheese is quite different. It might have already been stored unrefrigerated for days before it is mature. I have often eaten cheese when it is well past its sell by date – it just carries on maturing.

Miscellaneous items

Nuts can keep indefinitely if they are not allowed to germinate. I once had two Brazil nuts as a child which I still have today. They were brought back by one of my seafaring uncles. The nut case is about 4 inches across when it grows. One is untouched the other was nicely carved to enable me to see what is in it. In those days nuts were a Xmas treat and I slowly picked away at it until I could retrieve a nut. While writing this up I suddenly got to thinking if there are any left. Perhaps it was topped up, although I cannot recall when. I just tried one and it was delicious perhaps almost seventy years old?

Dried fruit, some can keep almost indefinitely, they just carry on drying.

Xmas cake/pudding, these will last until next Xmas at least. We now always spend Xmas with our children. Despite this someone always gives us a Christmas package containing the usual. I have just finished off the cake which is about three months old. And I am looking forward to the next Christmas pudding – purchased well after Xmas when the price had gone down.

Supermarket Discards

The current practice seems to be that as soon as any items have reached their 'best before' date they are just dumped into the same skip as all the other rubbish. This is a criminal waste of food. With current legislation I would not place any blame on the supermarkets but I found it very sad when I read about the case of an employee who was instantly dismissed when he was caught keeping some of the discards to take home when he had finished work.

This practice was not always in force. I have a friend who has a smallholding where he once kept pigs. He had an agreement with some supermarkets that he would collect all their food discards. His first stop on the way home was to drop a selection off at the homes of some of the local pensioners. Then he would sort out some for his own family needs and the rest was fed to the pigs.

I can well remember leaning on a fence with Derek feeding his pigs. The only problem was taking all the plastic wrappers off the food and it took some practice to get up to speed. Of course one of the reasons why it took me so long was that I took at least a one bite sample of the wide variety of food the pigs were eating. There was not even the slightest hint of mould on the bread and the sausage rolls and meat pies were perfectly edible and there was plenty of cake for afters!

Restaurant Discards

One again I would like to ban all **Two for the Price of One** adverts. This seems to be increasing, until there are very few pub meals without them. It distinguishes between a sole member of the public and others who eat in groups. Why not just an advert which says there will be a price reduction for one person only.

It was very refreshing to be in Northern Spain during my Camino. There hardly anything was wasted. Not that I ever left anything, I was ravenous after a good days walking. But there were those that did, and it was recycled to the pigs and poultry as soon as it left the plates.

Not so now in the UK, where outlets seem to compete to keep up with the ones next door. Particularly with the two for one 'mixed grills'. Inevitably one person likes this but will not touch some of the other items on the menu and the other will select different items to discard. At the end of the meal there is a lot of high protein left over. Chips are another one where they seem to compete to satisfy the hungriest customer. They could serve a more reasonable amount of chips with extra for the big appetite. It is not unusual for a third of the meal to be left.

Discards in General.

There seems to be a general 'health and safety issue' which prevents supermarket and restaurants being able to recycle the way Derek did not so long ago. These need revising to enable animal and poultry to get a more balanced diet. There are many parts of the county where this would work a treat just as it does in some parts of Europe.

ADVERTISING

In October 2011 Harry Wallop, the retail editor of the Daily Telegraph reported on a new approach to advertising developed by Nestle for its Purina pet food. The advert was already being shown on Austrian television.

To a human viewer it would just look, and sound like, any other pet food advert. However dogs, like many animals hear sounds over a wider range of frequencies than humans. The advert includes sounds and calls which only the dog can hear; these alert the dog to the advert – which ideally responds by wagging its tail.

The gullible owner then goes out to buy the product their pet has responded to; paying an inflated price for the pet food so that the manufacturer can recover the costs of developing such a sophisticated advert.

Sadly, advertising it here to stay

We are inundated by adverts in every field of the media. I would categorise them into two distinct ways;

Advertisements for Coming Events

I can see nothing wrong with advertising for coming events – how else could we be informed. Whether it is a pop concert in your locality or the excellent TV series Foyle's War.

There are other events, such as the warning issued just before a tax return is due to make sure you do not get penalised. Others are to remind us that the tax free saving account ISA, is coming to an end in a few months time.

I suppose that the first few times a new product is launched that could be acceptable. The rest of them I have an issue with.

Advertisements for advertising's sake

The introduction of colour supplements meant that colour advertisements could be used for the first time.

Ever since the start of the advertising channels on television the advertising content has been going up and up, and up, each year. Now I never watch anything on an advertising channel live; I simply record it and play it back later when I can run through the adverts without having to watch any of them.

Some TV adverts have been around a long time; beans and cereal adverts come to mind. I remember reading about nappies adverts – over 30% of the final product price was in television adverts. I suppose by now they are advertising for the new disposable nappies. 'Disposable' comes down to you and me again, when we pay extra for the sewage charges because they clog up the drains.

With such high charges for advertisements, when will the gullible public learn not to be conned? If they realised that, whatever the advert, it is almost certainly cheaper with own brands where there is no extra cost for advertising. Sometimes they will be made on the same production lines with a different label. Now when I know that something is being advertised on the television I will deliberately look around for a substitute which is just as good.

THE ANIMAL WORLD

I doubt that anyone could sensibly argue that, as the human race takes up more and more land for agriculture, there is less and less available for flora and fauna to carry on evolving the way they have done since life began on this planet.

For me this is very sad. I can remember that, when I was at school, the atlas we used still had a few blotches on it that were labelled 'unexplored'. I now appreciate that 'unexplored' did not mean the absence of human beings; it simply meant that no Europeans had been there. We now know that there were people in these regions but they were hunter gatherers who lived in harmony with their environment and if over- population threatened that harmony they would kill each other in tribal warfare, just as the North American Indians once did, until a balance was restored.

I have always been fascinated by the 'natural world'. I was a sickly child; suffering from asthma and bronchitis. My mother told me that when I was ill one of the ways she could keep me occupied for hours was by sitting me by a window to watch the birds in the garden. When I was well enough to venture into the garden she was forever trying to stop me eating the worms I found. On reflection maybe she should have left me alone. Worms are very nutritious and protein was in short supply during the war.

I am not sure that I can actually remember those very early days but I do recall the years that followed when I became an observer, keeper and collector of all sorts of things. I would watch the frogs spawn in the spring before taking a sample to watch them develop. I even tried keeping an ants nest but my biggest mistake was bringing home a tawny owl chick. I became a dab hand at catching newts; I never needed a net, just a stick with a bit of string on the end to attach a worm to. One day when I had no string I improvised with a long reed which worked just as well.

I collected leaves, flowers, butterflies and, I must confess, birds eggs. The latter frequently involved climbing for which I had neither the equipment nor training and on reflection I was probably very lucky to survive intact. I managed to reach my first sparrow hawk nest at the age of twelve. It was over halfway up a vertical pine tree with no branches to grip until the last couple of meters before the nest. The old quarries where the doves nested were even riskier and it was a couple of years later when I literally 'went out on a limb' to reach my first rook nest. I had studied it for a while before deciding that if the last thin branch broke it would not snap off so that as long as I held on I would just fall to one of the lower stronger branches. I normally only ever took one egg from a nest.

I also did my share of hunting and gathering for food. I learned that taking the first clutch of eggs from a lapwing nest might do more good than harm. They would always lay another clutch soon after, when the grass was a little bit taller and provided more cover from predators. Of course in those days they were a very common bird with up to a dozen pairs in a single large field. The mallard duck also provided a tasty change from hen's eggs. A clutch would normally consist of at least ten eggs and taking two or three was never noticed. The only edible fungi I knew of then was the mushroom and I bought back plenty during the autumn. Brown trout were always appreciated whenever I could catch them.

When books are discussed, people often reflect on what they read when they were young. I often have little to contribute to such conversations; I have heard of most of the authors they discuss but I never read any of the books. I read books on topics such as chess and I was seldom without a library book on some aspect of wildlife.

I am a member of many national wildlife organisations and active with local groups. Now I would gladly help to put away people who are obsessed with collecting the eggs of some of our rarest birds and would never consider collecting some of the things I used to. I also do my own projects – often without permission! The end of the lane I live in is bordered by an open field and there was once only a single hawthorn bush to contrast with the barbed wire. Now there are two Scots pines and a silver birch to break up an almost continuous hedge of buddleia and honeysuckle. In front of the hedge are daffodils and crocuses.

I seem to have a bit of an obsession with planting honeysuckle and there are other lanes where I have given nature a helping hand. I have often been told how pleasant they smell which is completely lost on me since my sense of smell was diminishing long before I started smoking. My main motive is to provide habitat for one of our most spectacular and rare insects – the elephant hawk moth. The first time I saw one I thought it must be an escapee humming bird!

Those are my credentials for offering solutions to some of the threats to biodiversity on this planet. The long term ideal solutions are to educate and reduce the human population. Many of the following ideas are therefore 'short term fixes', at least I hope so.

Endangered Species

Most of the creatures that have ever lived on this planet are already extinct and it is inevitable that more will follow them. The natural counterbalance to this is for more creatures to evolve and this is still taking place. However it takes much longer for a new species to evolve than it does to accelerate the extinction of an existing one.

Man has been the sole cause of accelerating the extinction of many creatures in many different ways including the destruction of habitat, the introduction of alien species and overhunting for food or other animal parts.

My own views on some of the measures being taken to retain some of our most spectacular wildlife are as follows.

Horned and Tusked Animals

I switched to writing this section of the book after reading that rhino horn was regarded as the latest cure for cancer; by rich Asians of course, in this case mainly Vietnamese. My strange mind immediately asked the question "what if this claim was correct?"

I reflected on other 'very natural' products for other human problems. I first heard of Spanish fly being used as an aphrodisiac when I was a youth at sea. I can recall some of the stories and jokes I was told.

I now know that it is made from a green beetle which is dried and crushed to a powder and has been around since Roman times.

When I checked it up on the net I was amazed at the number of adverts from suppliers and also found out that it is currently being given to some domestic animals. I concluded that it must work although it is not without potential problems.

Back to the 'latest cancer cure'; it is doubtful if any acceptable, reproducible scientific tests will be carried out on rhino horn in the immediate future but these may not be necessary for desperate people worldwide, with money, to clutch at one 'last straw'. Since rhino horn is such a natural product it is very unlikely to do them any harm and a few thousand pounds or even a few tens of thousands of pounds will not be an obstacle to many people.

Currently there are two main reasons for the already ridiculous high prices being paid for rhino horn. The first is for ornamental use. Various very attractive adornments can be carved from horn. Many of the worst culprits are in the Middle East, particularly in Yemen were it is used to make the handle for the jambiya, the short dagger that is worn on the leg adjacent to the calf. In theory it is used for personal protection and can come in very handy during a sword fight when blades are locked at shoulder height with one hand, a quick thrust from a jambiya to the abdomen with the other hand will end it. In reality anyone who can afford such an adornment is very unlikely to ever do his own fighting but it will demonstrate his status in his society.

The second use is in Chinese medicine were small quantities of powdered horn are one of the ingredients used in medicines for treating a variety of ailments including fever, rheumatism and gout. There has been some limited scientific research in this area – by the Chinese who concluded that the small quantities of horn involved could not possibly have any effect. However with medicine just like with religion it is very difficult to expose myths that have been around for more than a thousand years and there will always be some 'positive feedback' due to placebo effects.

Researching the price of rhino horn is interesting and confusing because there is never any firm agreed data for a 'closed market'. One fact I have managed to glean is that the price of Asian horn is much higher than for African horn, sometimes twice as high. The current 'market' prices may be over £50,000/kg, presumably for the Asian horn.

There is far more data for the weight of an African horn; at two years old it is about 1 kg but an adult horn can be over 4 kg. The price for a single animal can therefore easily reach £100,000.

A poacher will only receive a small fraction of this but that is often sufficient to exceed what he might earn in a year of honest work. In between the poacher and the end market there is a tree of middle men who take little risk in making fat profits. Some middle men are now financing poachers by providing them with increasingly sophisticated weapons and equipment to make their kills.

I have some sympathy with the poacher. His motivation may be the family he is responsible for looking after, or ridding himself of the debts he has been lured into. I have no sympathy with the rest of them and in an ideal world they would be the ones who should be hit hardest. In the real world they are business men with other interests who can cover their backs and hire 'smart' lawyers if they are investigated.

As in any war the humble foot soldier is the easiest target but without him a ground war cannot be pursued. Risk assessment is something everyone must do at sometime – including a poacher. The risks, and punishments, including instant death must be escalated to act as a deterrent.

Whether the latest 'cancer cure', which might require larger amounts of powder increases demand further or not, the price is already high enough to threaten the survival of the species. At the time of writing this there are still five distinct species of rhino. Two are in Africa and the other three in Southern Asia. Because of their proximity to the markets, the higher cost/kg and the lack of well funded game reserves within easy reach of the tourists, the Asian rhinos are the ones threatened with extinction.

Practical Solutions

It is with a very heavy heart that I am making some of the following suggestions although I am confident that they could work. Many people who have a genuine but often misguided love of animals might be very upset with what I have to say. However if we have to wait until the poor are no longer poor and the uneducated educated all we will be left with is some nice pictures and wildlife films.

Start up Rhino farms

With illicit rhino horn bringing such high prices, the market could be supplied with legal rhino horn to bring the price down. It would clearly be a very economic enterprise to farm rhinos – there would be no problem with funding. Market forces would ensure that the Asian species would be a priority.

Once the first farms were established the scientific methods developed for other branches of animal husbandry would accelerate production. Artificial insemination, increasing the number of calves per birth and it may even be possible for an African rhino to be implanted with a fertilised egg from the closely related Asian species.

There is no reason why farms need to be established in the area where the rhinos are endemic; any country where they could tolerate the climate and the food they need could be grown might be suitable. Within a few decades farms would be producing animals with higher horn to body mass ratios and far more calves than the remaining wild ones. Unless the 'cancer cure' is real the price will have crashed and the incentive for killing wild animals diminished.

Any farm should pay a tax on the profits they make which should be used to fund game wardens that are looking after the remaining wild animals. They should always be better trained and equipped than their adversaries.

Farming Precedents

The mink has now been farmed for its fur for many years. Before then they were trapped in the wild during the winter months when the fur was in its best condition. One of the many means of killing them was the grotesque gin trap. Even when more humane traps were used they frequently had to be left for long periods during prolonged spells of bad weather when the animals would suffer terrible deaths. The advent of mink farms reduced the cost of the fur and made it far less attractive to hunt for them in the wild.

There are sad lessons to be learned from mink farming. They should have been restricted to either areas where they were indigenous or on islands where any escapees could be contained. However it was very difficult to foresee people being stupid enough to deliberately release them into the UK countryside where they have caused havoc. Now there are even some close to where I live which is a long way from any of the farms where they were originally released.

A far better solution of course is to satisfy female vanity with coats made from artificial fur. I am far from being an expert in this field but I understand that very few people can spot the difference. To avoid moral chastisement they could be fitted with a label and slogan such as "my coat is artificial" but somehow I can not see that happening.

Crocodile farming is legal and productive in many parts of the world and I have seen several crocodile farms in Thailand. Although many people only think in terms of the skins which are used for shoes and handbags they are a good example of a farmed animal where nothing is wasted; some cuts of meat are as good as any of the traditional beef, lamb etc, and the eggs are delicious.

A less well known example of wild animal farming is at the Sriracha tiger zoo in Thailand. There are over a hundred acres of land where a variety of birds, reptiles and animals are kept in very reasonable conditions compared with some other zoos I have been to. It is only an hour or so by coach from the popular tourist resort of Pattaya and even closer to the office where I worked for many months.

I always try an avoid being part of an organised trip which rushes people around to make sure they see and photograph 'everything' in the allotted time span. I prefer to arrive just when they are opening and then be one of the last ones to be asked to leave. After my first visit I had still not explored the full complex and I had a lot of questions to ask so I went back again. I spoke to as many employees as I could which was much easier when the official parties where elsewhere and many of them were just relaxing while waiting for the next group.

The star attractions of the zoo, as the name suggests, are the Bengal tigers. There are over 200 of them – far more than necessary to sustain the population and provide animals for the shows. They had a very active breeding program which went to lengths I would not have thought possible. They had females that were producing over five cubs from a single pregnancy. To make sure that she would soon be carrying again the cubs were taken away soon after birth and then passed to a pig which acted as a surrogate mother. The keepers were very proud of this and keen to answer any questions – except for one – "with such an exploding tiger population where do they all finish up?"

The only hesitant answer that I was given was "exporting them to other zoos worldwide". There is no doubt that many of them might end up in other zoos but that market would be a limited one because of the high cost of their upkeep in food and satisfactory enclosures.

The next time I was in the office I decided to continue with my enquiries. It was not something I could carry out myself because although English was the official office language which some of the Thais had mastered there were others who I found it very difficult to discuss anything with. I therefore turned to Phon, my right hand woman for such situations, to ask everyone in the office a few simple questions; had they been to the zoo, what did they think of the tiger breeding programme and where did they think the surplus tigers finished up?

Most of them had been to the zoo but had never thought about what they had seen and had no idea where any surplus tigers might end up which surprised me. I later put the same questions to all the Europeans I knew who had been there and most of them had similar reactions to the Thai staff in the office. It was several days later (sufficient time for him to make his own enquiries), when one of the more astute lads in the office who also spoke good English came over to me and said "I understand why you asked the questions Bill, and yes, you are right – the tigers finish up in China."

The Thai 'tiger farm' is not 'legal' and no doubt there are officials and middle men who are making big money from it. However it might just take a little pressure off the noble animals still fortunate enough to be in the wild. If more such farms were built the price of tiger parts would be reduced and take more pressure off those in the wild and, unlike the rhino where only the horn is of significant value, every part of the tiger seems to be used. (The male sex organs are very highly valued, in Chinese medicine.)

Horn Removals

Another deterrent to poaching is to ensure that there is little of any value on the rhinos horn. As soon as the horns reach a commercial size they could be removed and replaced with artificial horns. There is a wide range of metallic and none metallic materials available today that could be used to produce a horn with the same strength and weight as a real horn. There are a variety of ways they could be attached to the remaining base. They would have a surface finish coloured to be a close match with real horn. Tourists would never notice the difference but the locals would know and so would any potential poachers.

The artificial horns would need to be replaced or modified from time to time until the animal reached maturity. This would mean the development of a new, highly specialised, branch of engineering but no more challenging today than the one farriers faced when they first shod horses. It would be expensive to start up, but could also be profitable if the horns removed were legally sold.

The Ivory Trade.

One of the most stupid and disgusting events I can recall was the burning of poached African elephant tusks on the orders of the Kenyan president Mwai Kibaki in July 2011. There were 335 tusks together with more than 40,000 ivory carvings weighing more than five tons.

The event was termed the 'first national celebration of African Elephant Law Enforcement Day'. It was spectacular and covered by the media worldwide which provide a lot of publicity for the president.

Ivory is a beautiful material which has certainly been used since the days of the first Egyptian Pharaohs and probably long before then. In more recent times it was used for the first billiard balls. There are enormous worldwide stocks in various forms – all held quite legally. There are now many substitute materials which are far superior for some application, for example billiard, snooker and pool balls. However I can not foresee the demand for new ivory ever being sated.

The elephant is not an endangered species throughout the African continent although there may be some areas where it is threatened such as Zimbabwe where members of the government are probably involved in the poaching. To counterbalance threatened areas there are others where parks are overpopulated with elephants and they are destroying the habitat for other species. I have been fortunate enough to visit the Kruger national park in South Africa and by chance I managed to find a bar, not normally used by tourists, where some of the wardens drank in the evenings.

I remember telling them that I had watched a very young elephant knocking over a small tree of about five inches in diameter at the base. By the time the tree was leaning at an angle where it could easily reach the few sparse leaves at the top it never bothered and just started to attack another small tree. It appeared to be just practicing for the day when it would be strong enough to fell much bigger trees with more worthwhile pickings.

That sparked off a very interesting conversation. They told me that elephant damage to trees was already threatening the habitat of other animals and something needed to be done about the problem to restore a natural balance. The options were transporting animals – ideally whole herds – to other parks, and selective culling. The first solution is incredibly expensive and the second one political dynamite. They had no idea which option would be used but suspected that neither of them would be implemented and the destruction would continue.

All elephants eventually die and there is a continuous natural supply of tusks without any culling or poaching. Why not use this beautiful material?

Back to president Kibaki – what did his spectacular bonfire achieve? A lot of ivory was removed from the illicit market which would certainly increase the price and make poaching more worthwhile. A lot of fine material and ornaments were destroyed. He claimed his motive was to put his country at the forefront of wildlife conservation. If true it was a very inspiring and noble motive but sadly it was a very misguided one.

The alternative would have been to sell it and reduce demand which would make poaching less attractive and plough the proceeds back into conservation projects including providing long distance sniper rifles for wardens.

Conservation in the UK

There are probably very few places in the world without national and local conservation issues. They may not be as spectacular and newsworthy as some of the international problems but the important difference is that we can all make a direct contribution in some way.

Fortunately all is not doom and gloom for once; a lot has already been achieved in educating young people about their local wildlife. Yesterday six of us (including two children) spent about three hours erecting bird, bat and hedgehog boxes in a new nature reserve which effectively starts where the 'honey suckle/buddleia hedge I planted years ago ends.

Many schools which still have some land that has not been sold off to developers have their own wildlife areas and about 3 miles from where I live is a very special school, purpose built for residential courses in the village of Kingswood. Kids from schools all over the region can go and stay there for a week of outward bound type of activities and wildlife projects. Their website **Kingswood.co.uk** is well worth a visit. As a 'friend of Kingswood' I get called in from time to time to clear paths and scrub, plant trees and hedges etc. I even managed to erect some house martin nest boxes under an overhang overlooking a play area when the staff were 'not looking' – I have never passed the test to qualify me to use my own ladder!!

There is probably something going on near where the reader lives and if not, why not start something? A word of warning about the latter; wildlife is a bandwagon everyone seems to want to be associated with. It is sometimes amazing how many people there are who want to talk about it but far fewer who are prepared to get their hands dirty.

National Organisations

Many national organisations have seen incredible growth since I first joined them, which is very positive. However growth can have its down side. The more money there is around the more attractive organisations become for professional organisers and fund raisers. The hard sell techniques of the retail industry have taken over as each organisation competes for funds.

As with any charity they get worse as Xmas approaches. Now there are books of raffle tickets which the recipient is meant to feel obliged to sell. I am not the sort of person who feels comfortable pressurising friends and acquaintances to buy any sort of tickets. The first time this happened I bought the lot myself; since then I just recycle the paper along with the junk mail.

The Hawk and Owl trust have always had a very 'personal touch' sales technique – I get a report each year on what has happened in 'my box' together with a form to pay for the first years subscription as a present for a friend who they hope will become a new member. I look forward to reading about my box and pass on details to other people but I am not prepared to pressurise them into joining.

I have two friends who I see regularly who are very active in the RSPB; organising as well as taking part in field trips and meetings. I am a relatively inactive member who joins them when work on local sites is needed. I rarely go on 'spotting and counting' trips because I have so little to contribute. I get a lot of pleasure out of listening to bird songs but have great difficulty in distinguishing one from another and many of the small birds I see I can only describe as 'another little brown job'.

Whenever I am in the company of members of the RSPB one topic which regularly crops up is the internal politics in the organisation. I suppose this is inevitable since the organisation has grown significantly since I first joined.

The deer 'problem'

There are now six species of deer which are now well established in the wild in the UK. The Red and the Roe are the only two with a claim to be truly indigenous although the Fallow has been around since they were intentionally introduced by the Normans. The Sitka, Muntjac and Chinese Water Deer are all relatively new 'alien species'. Some may have been deliberately released; others were simply escapees from deer parks and private collections. They remained local to areas where they started off until the population expanded to the point where they needed more space. The expansion of the Sitka was easy to observe and document because it is the second largest deer in the UK after the Red.

The expansion of the Muntjac and Chinese Water Deer was not so easy to observe. Both are relatively small and secretive, seldom grazing in' open spaces. The Chinese Water Deer is only about half a metre to the shoulder weighing no more than about 11 kg. An unusual feature is that the male has tusks similar to a wild boar rather than the antlers sported by the other species. I have never seen one but I have caught glimpses of the Muntjac crossing roads and tracks on Cannock Chase which is not very far from where I live.

One thing all the species of deer in the UK have in common is that they have no natural predators to maintain a balanced population. This has resulted in population explosions and conflicts between farmers and foresters. There are many crops which are far more attractive to deer than grass and they will strip the bark and kill all but the most mature of many varieties of tree.

One solution used is the deer fence which is intended to keep them out of farmers' fields and areas of newly planted trees. These are expensive to install and difficult to maintain intact particularly across land with a steep incline; deer will soon find and use any breach in a fence.

If deer fences were totally effective; what then? Herds would have a restricted gene pool making them vulnerable to disease and in winter they would face starvation. There is only one practical solution and that is to control the population by selective killing.

Cull/Kill

The dictionary definition of the term cull is to control an animal population by selective killing of some of the group and has been increasingly used during my lifetime. It has become a very emotive term and the execution of a cull is normally planned well in advance of the event. This gives time for the various interested parties to discuss it and the more extreme animal rights activists time to try and disrupt it.

Only trained marksmen will be involved who will be paid for their work and which, together will the appeals and legal work, can make culling very expensive.

It should never be necessary for deer. Controlling the deer population should be an ongoing practice which would go on unnoticed by the general public and generate funds for local economies rather than costing money.

Precedents for this have been have been established for many years in the highlands of Scotland. There, together with fishing and shooting game birds, killing deer is the lifeblood of many rural areas.

A couple of years ago I spent a week in a small highland village. It was a male only family gathering and apart from one fruitless day's fishing we were only there for the hill walking and the beer. There was only one village watering hole which was in the bar of a hotel. Some evenings my group of five made up the majority of clients. I took advantage of the opportunity to meet other people using the bar who were frequently on their own.

The locals I met were all in the tourist industry; the visitors I met were all there for the deer stalking. They had often had blank days without firing a single shot which was expensive because they were always with a local guide. One evening one of them was very pleased with himself when he announced that he had just 'bagged' a couple of hinds. His extra cost for a successful day was more than I had paid for a week in the cottage we stayed in.

At the end of our stay there my party were all agreed on one thing – without the fishing, shooting and deer stalking, the hotel and bar would close within weeks and the village would quickly become a ghost town as the locals were forced to move away to find work or live out the rest of their lives on state benefits.

There is no reason why the Highland approach should not be used in other regions of the UK. Many of the people who shoot in Scotland actually live in the South East of England. Their 'carbon footprint' would be improved if they did not travel as far for some of their hunting trips. It would be in no one's interest to over kill and the general public would still be able to enjoy watching deer as they do now.

Canada Geese

This is one of the largest members of the goose family and it is unlikely that the reader will never have seen one. Large numbers migrate from Scandinavia to spend the winter in the UK. They are truly wild and spend the winter on grasslands and marshes well away from towns and cities. Many of these are legally shot by wildfowlers.

The Canada Geese that have become a problem are those which are resident all year round in the UK where they live in parks and recreational grassland such as playing fields. I do not need to go very far to see examples of where they have become a pest. One is in West Park in the centre of Wolverhampton. When I first took my children there I never saw any, but on my most recent visit there I could easily imagine that I was on a goose farm.

Another example is in the village of Perton where they first took up residence around a small lake on the edge of the village. Now their droppings are a health threat to children playing on any grassed areas and they wander around the gardens of houses where they vary their diet by eating flowers and ornamental plants. In both these examples the problem is exacerbated by people feeding them. When I visited West Park there was an elderly gentleman of Indian origin who had a bin liner full of bread and cakes to feed them.

All the people involved with maintaining amenities seem to be agreed that the population needs to be controlled. I know a drinking acquaintance who once worked at West Park and one of his jobs was to prick the eggs in any nest he found; that does not seem to have worked.

Once a colony of Canada Geese is established, other less aggressive species of birds suffer a decline and may be eliminated altogether in some cases. It is in everyone's interest to maintain a bio-diverse balance of birds in our parks and recreational areas.

This is clearly a case for organised culls. The geese are almost tame with no fear of human beings and could be netted or driven into cages where they could be dispatched just as humanely as the domestic geese that are reared for Xmas dinners. There would be no shortage of volunteers to assist an 'expert' and the cull should make a profit when the birds are marketed. The timing of any cull should be unannounced and take place at dawn when few people are around.

A Canada Goose has far less fat than a domestic one and is an excellent source of protein. The younger birds can be roasted and the tougher older birds would make much healthier curries than the ones made from intensively reared chickens which I tend to call 'plastic chickens'.

Of course there will always be people who are against killing any form of wildlife; such people seem to have a far greater love of their own misguided correctness than a love of wildlife. There is even a Canada Goose Preservation Society whose members claim that culling is cruel, ineffective and expensive. Some of their alternative methods of controlling the population would certainly be ineffective and expensive. Methods could easily be compared by trying their solutions in one area and mine in another similar area.

Marine Conservation

This is a worldwide issue rather than one confined to the UK or the EU. However like so many issues we should put our own house in order before trying to tell other countries what they should be doing.

Commercial fishing

I had never heard of Hugh Fearnley-Whittingstall until I read about his 'Fish Fight'. At last someone had taken up an issue that had been annoying me for years and I immediately passed it on to everyone on my E mail list encouraging them to sign his petition.

Fish stocks, particularly in the North Sea, had been devastated by years of overfishing and a quota system had been introduced which was intended to solve the problem. Politicians introduce legislation which all too frequently is not thought through and the consequences considered. This was one of the worst, or should I say best, examples ever.

Individual species of fish are seldom found alone in isolated areas and often shoals of more than one species will be mixed up together. Individual boats were allocated quotas for specific species and anything which was caught which did not fit into their quota had to be returned to the sea. This sounds wonderful in principle if the unwanted fish could be returned to the water the way an angler can. The practicality of commercial fishing by hook, net or trawl means that by the time they are taken on board and sorted most of them are dead!

An EU estimate for the proportion of fish discarded was between 40% and 60% of a typical catch and very few of them would be alive. The dead fish could be categorized in a number of ways, for example undersized and above minimum size limits. If the target catches are herring the size of the mesh is designed to allow undersized fish to pass through but will still catch undersized fish of larger species such as cod and haddock.

The most important categorization is between high priced 'popular' fish such as cod, haddock, plaice and sole and 'other fish'. The reader only has to look at the prices in the window of any fishmongers shop or the fish counter at any supermarket to appreciate why any fisherman would want to make sure they fulfilled their quota for the prime species even if their last catches included a very high percentage of 'other fish'. If they have a 'good day' on their last day and catch too many of their target fish even these must be discarded until they are down to their quota.

Some of the 'other fish' could be landed legally since there is normally no quota involved, but the low prices do not make it worthwhile to sort them out. These include mackerel, whiting, gurnard, coley, pollock, pouting and flounder.

I have caught most of the above 'other fish' angling from the shore or from a boat and eaten them; while some might be more appetizing than others they all provided a good meal without the need for exotic sauces to disguise the taste. Hugh is doing a good job at making the public aware of alternative fish although he invariably includes an exotic sauce. Some of the recent immigrant populations who have eaten a wider variety of fish than the average Brit are also more likely to try something new.

One of the best examples of traditionally eating and not eating one of other fish in this country is the dogfish which is the commonest member of the shark family in British waters. In London it has always been marketed as rock salmon and is regarded as a prime fish in their fish and chip shops. I have never managed to find it in a chip shop outside London.

The alternative

At the time of writing new legislation is being 'discussed and considered' in countries throughout Europe through the EU. That may take some time and no one can be sure what form it might take.

What I would like to see is a **complete ban** on discharging **any dead fish or animals** (dolphins and seals may be drowned during netting) into the sea – it should be made a **criminal offence** with appropriate punishments for non compliance. Once a fishing boat has filled its holds with whatever it has caught it must return to port. Any part of a catch with no economic outlet for human consumption should be recycled as food for fish farms.

Conservation areas

An ideal conservation area is one with no commercial exploitation and which is only ever entered by humans as observers. Isolated conservation areas have been around for a long time in some parts of the UK and Europe. A few have been designated as such but the vast majority are natural – they are only conservation areas because of their remote locations or dangerous waters.

One of the smallest conservation areas I know of is off the Caribbean island of St Lucia. It covers less than an acre and is isolated with marker buoys to keep out the local fishermen. On a single night dive I ticked off more 'firsts' than on any other of my 300 or so dives. There was one strange creature which the local guides had never identified and suspected it might be an unclassified species.

At the time of writing there is a campaign in the UK to increase the number of designated sites in the UK by 127 and there are concerns that this small number may be cut back. Many of these sites are media eye catching sites involving a single species. The reader may have seen the television programmes about the sea horses in Poole Harbor in Dorset. There are conflicts of interest between yachtsmen and conservation groups. I know the area well because my son Alan who is very knowledgeable and involved with yachting lived nearby. There are compromise solutions which could satisfy both parties but the talking still goes on.

Some of my own ideas are far more radical than specifying a few dedicated areas. These originated in the late 1970's not too long after I first took up scuba diving. I took the family to Devon several times a year because my parents had retired to the small village of Malborough near Salcombe. Most days we visited one of the many beaches and coves nearby and I took the opportunity to have a dive. Sometimes I would just bring back items of interest to them such as a hermit crab or a starfish which were returned to the water as soon as the children had examined them. On other occasions I might have something for the table such as a crab.

I was diving off Slapton Sands one day. My dive plan was a very simple one – straight out to sea for a few hundred metres to keep well away from any of the beach anglers, then along the coast with any tide until my air supply dictated that it was time to head back to the beach where one of the kids would spot me and hurry over to see what I had in my 'goody bag'. I was halfway through my dive when I saw a strange mound ahead of me in the cloudy waters which seemed to be moving. As I approached I could see that it was a great heap of spider crabs with a diameter of nearly two metres and a height of about half a metre. I circled them a few times and then knelt on the bottom to watch them. There were hundreds of them and I quickly dismissed any thoughts of filling my bag. It was clearly a mass breeding frenzy and I felt very privileged to be observing it. I normally found spider crabs along rocky shore lines but these were in the centre of a very flat area with a sand and mud bottom. By the time I had finished watching them it was time to head back to the shore.

The next day I decided to repeat the same dive to see if I could locate the spider crabs again. I was less than half way out when I came to a cloudy area with such poor visibility that it was hardly worth diving. I carried on to find out if there were better conditions further out. There were, the water was suddenly clear again. I looked back to see a wall of cloud and I was starting to feel very apprehensive about this strange phenomenon. Then I heard the noise of an engine which was louder that the usual ones in that area and I decided to abort the dive and head back to the shore.

The trawl only missed me by a few meters as I finned as hard as I could back to safety. By the time the water was shallow enough to remove my fins and stand up I looked back and watched the trawler making another pass even closer to the beach; so close that the anglers were hurriedly hauling in their lines to prevent them being cut or, even worse, dragging their rods and reels into the sea. I have never been so angry. It is many years ago but I still feel angry just thinking about it.

I often wonder if I would have had any chance if the trawl had caught me; I still had a full bottle and a sharp knife. James Bond would have found it to be a minor irritation but I am not a fictional hero.

When I stopped thinking about myself I reviewed the whole event I had witnessed. I had often dived from that beach and marketable sized flatfish were few and far between; the anglers seldom seemed to catch anything – either I or one of the kids used to check on this whenever we visited the area and I have fished it myself. Now what haunts me most is the fate of that breeding mass of spider crabs. If the trawl had hit them they would have been smashed to bits.

I discussed what I had seen with some of the locals. Evidently there was nothing illegal about trawling close to the beach and it was not a one-off event. It might not be illegal but it should be.

An alternative approach

All coastal waters are a natural breeding ground for many creatures which spend most of their life further out to sea. We should be thinking in terms of making a continuous great conservation area around the coast with designated exceptions made for commercial activity, and not the other way round.

The conservation area should stretch from the shoreline to say half a mile from the coast. In some areas the shoreline is relatively easy to establish; there are others where it is not so easy such as Morecambe Bay where it varies throughout the year and the sand and mud banks exposed at low tide stretch for miles. Once agreed limits had been established anyone could locate them with map references and GPS systems and anyone at sea could report infringing vessels.

There should be exceptions to the general rule for activities such as crabbing and shrimping which need to be close to the coast. Angling should be allowed anywhere other than a few total exclusion zones. Fishing with a rod and line is a healthy pastime enjoyed by hundreds of thousands of people who eat what they take and return unwanted fish to the sea unharmed.

Think big and imagine an ideal scenario instead of just thinking in terms of bits and pieces.

Summary

There are many other issues which I thought of including. There is a lot to be optimistic about, particularly the way that so many schools are becoming involved with wildlife projects.

On the negative side there are too many organised groups that seem to be against any practical control measures that involve culling, and killing for sport is far worse to them. They are totally blind to the fact that without managed grouse moors there would soon be no grouse and no habitat for a variety of small birds that thrive on the same moors. The countryside in many areas, including the one around where I live, would be much more bland and monotonous if it were not for the copses and other areas set aside for releasing hand reared pheasants and partridges where syndicates can pay a lot of money for a day's shooting.

One of the most stupid of the 'anti groups' is the one campaigning against angling. Since I was a child I have witnessed the steady decline in the number of ponds in the countryside. They were mostly man made and used to provide water for livestock. Then farmers started to use more reliable piped water. The ponds were neglected and either weeded over and slowly died or were deliberately filled in with builders' rubble or more dubious waste. (The value of any hole in the ground has increased dramatically.)

The field ponds of the past provided a wonderful habitat for a variety of birds, amphibians, dragonflies, damselflies and many other creatures. Fortunately some of the habitats that have been lost have been replaced by new ponds and lakes to cater for anglers. Anglers have also been one of the main groups responsible for cleaning up rivers and canals. No 'anti' group would have had either the money or inclination to carry out this type of work. I have met many anglers over the years and know some of them very well. They are invariably very knowledgeable about the wildlife in our waterways and get a lot of pleasure observing it when the fish are not interested in their bait or lure. I have never met any of the anti groups but I doubt if any of them would appreciate real nature as the anglers do.

THE ENERGY CRISIS

This is one of the topics in this book where few people would challenge my claim to be something of an 'expert.'

I was first introduced to the efficient use of energy as a 17 year old when I studied the now dated subject of 'heat engines'. As a student at university it had become thermodynamics and was taught at a much higher and more academic level. When I became employed in the academic world I taught traditional subjects such as thermodynamics and heat transfer to honours degree level. I was also involved with developing and teaching broader applied subjects for the Building Services and Agricultural Engineering fields.

Energy efficiency was always a consideration during both my full time work and my consultancy work in industry. I therefore have a very practical as well as an academic background to fall back on. As a result of this I have been a co-author and a sole author of two technical books which have contributed to increasing engineering knowledge of many complex topics in the field of saving energy.

Now I keep up to date with current developments and discussions by reading the Professional Engineer (PE) , which is the magazine for IMechE members, as well as what I see and read in the media. Some of the articles and the discussions in the PE are of course on a much higher level than those in parliament or the media because they are written by and for people who understand the fundamentals.

I am probably in a very good position to write yet another book on the energy crisis. However I am taking up the challenge of trying to summarise the basic facts that anyone without a scientific or engineering background can understand. To help them to see through all the bullshit that is repeated ad nauseam by politicians and the media.

The mistakes that politicians have made, and continue to make, are going to affect us all; perhaps far sooner than many people realise.

An Optimistic Note

One of the few optimistic notes in this chapter is the way the world has dealt with refrigerants. I published my first technical book in 1992 (Longman Group UK and is still available today – Eastop & Watson). Already the refrigeration industry was in turmoil. The most common refrigerants at the time of writing were chlorofluorocarbons (CFCs) which are known to be damaging the Earth's ozone layer.

In 1987 the Montreal Protocol agreement to limit the production of CFCs was signed by 24 countries. It is interesting to note that all the consumption of CFCs was in the northern hemisphere but one of the main effects was in the southern hemisphere. Today we know a lot more about the behaviour of the upper atmosphere. The USA were the main users of refrigeration but eventually they came on board.

There is now a general improvement in the ozone layers in both the southern hemisphere and the northern hemisphere. This demonstrates how we can save the planet provided there is a united action.

As well as covering conventional refrigerants in use at the time the book covers less well known refrigerant systems. These have been increasing used for industry and commercial buildings since the ban on CFCs.

I was on a reunion with some former building services students when one of the students looked up in the sky and pointed to a new development. He said he had used a source of waste heat to drive the air conditioning system. I felt good and it all seemed worthwhile writing the book.

Carbon dioxide emissions

This is without doubt one of the most important issues facing the world today. I will split this up into three main sections; Electrical Power Loads, Domestic Heating Loads and Transportation.

Electrical Power Loads

These can be further divided into; base loads and intermittent loads.

Base loads

This is the minimum base load which occurs at night. During this time the most efficient means of energy conversions can be kept running. Base loads include the following;

Nuclear

The UK has 16 reactors currently producing about 19% of its electrical load. In the late 1990s it contributed 25%. This has gradually declined as old plants are decommissioned and not replaced by new ones.

France has the highest proportion of nuclear reactors in its grid with about 80%. Japan needs to import about 84% of its energy requirements. It was a late starter because of Hiroshima and Nagasaki and its first nuclear power station came on line in about 1966. By the summer of 2011 it increased its capacity to 30% and had plans for it to go even higher.

Then came the disaster when a tsunami, hit their shores in October 2011. Fukushima was one of the worst hit and they also had key nuclear plants in the way and 19,000 people were killed. The plants were situated there because of the cheap cooling water supplies – the sea.

Japan had contingency plans for smaller tsunami but not for the magnitude of the one that struck Fukushima. It was a world setback and it gave the anti-nuclear lobby an excuse to cut back on their own programmes.

We should increase our nuclear capacity now. It is the only reliable, proven means of satisfying our grid and there are no carbon dioxide emissions involved. Once the UK led the world in the design of reactors, sadly our engineers have been decommissioning our old designs and are now too old and retired. They have not been replaced by new engineers. In the immediate future we will rely on an American design and a French design. There is no option until we can train our own staff again.

The new generation of reactors will be much more efficient and use up far more of the uranium fuel than the old ones they will be replacing. There is currently a lot of research in using alternatives to uranium as a fuel. One of the possibilities is using lithium. The next generation of fission power stations could well use lithium which has environmental advantages.

Tidal Power 1

The La Rance Barrage in France is the world's first tidal power station and was opened in 1966. It relies of the high tides of the Northern Hemisphere when they are accentuated by the surrounding land mass which produces even higher tides than normal. The barrage is located in the river Rance. It is still operating; it produces no carbon dioxide and is an economic success in terms of providing a contribution to the French national grid.

The UK has a far better potential which could replace three conventional power stations and make a significant contribution to our grid – about 6%. The Severn estuary produces a rise and fall of about14 m, second only to the Bay of Fundy in Canada. Feasibility studies have been carried out well before I was a student and the latest is still ongoing.

If carried out, it will be about twice a costly as nuclear or a conventional power station. Once it has been paid for, the running costs will be minimal and it should last a lifetime. The barrage would consist of a span linking the Welsh coast with the English coast. This should have been carried out years ago but once again it comes down to politics.

One excuse is the environmental impact it will have on wildlife. For the fish population, salmon and eels will be carried by ladders at convenient locations. The bird population, there will be some pluses and some minuses. New habitats will be created for birds to compensate for any losses.

Tidal Power 2

There are rises and falls in the tides in the UK throughout the year – twice per day. These are much smaller than produced above; however in theory they could satisfy our needs for the entire grid. Unlike a barrage type dam they are continuously changing directions. They are also limited to about the first 5 m, below that, as any scuba diver will know, the sea will become relatively calm.

In 1974 Steven Salter introduced the concept of a nodding duck. The duck was to be on the surface of the water with a shape to allow the axis of rotation to be converted into energy production. It also had the effect of a calming the sea after it had passed through the wave. It was never commercially viable.

Currently there are lot of new ideas with commercial sponsorship centred at the Edinburgh University. These rely on underwater turbines. Some are designed to track the changing directions of the tide. The problems they face are much the same as oil rigs which have to cater for the highest winter storms which can rip the rig away if it is not suitably anchored to the sea bed. The cost of sufficiently engineered foundations has to be weighed against the cost of the energy produced.

We should carry on with these experiments but they are unlikely to produce any significant contribution to the grid in the near future.

Coal

Coal now currently contributes about 29% to the national grid. I can remember when it was about 80%. We should not cut back on coal until it can be replaced with a reliable source of energy such as nuclear. The existing power stations can be cleaned up to reduce the sulphur emissions. We have enough coal to last for hundreds of years but we now lack the miners to dig it up. The UK should open a few pits at a time and reconsider open cast mining. We should never be dependant on foreign coal.

Natural Gas.

Natural gas currently contributes about 41% the national grid. During the 1980's and early 1990's there was a dash for gas. The UK always had some gas from coal burn during an incomplete combustion process that produced coke and gas. It was used as lighting, domestic home use and certain industrial processes. It was never burnt in a national grid power station; it was much more economic to use coal directly.

Suddenly it was economic to use gas fired power stations; we squandered a precious resource that should have been used more wisely. It is ideally suited for co-generation schemes and district heating. Now we can no longer produce enough gas to satisfy our current needs and will have to import it. Russian gas is currently the cheapest; but would we like to rely on it? Some of their pipelines pass through other countries and there are security issues without being dictated to by Moscow.

Shale Gas Fracking.

"Shale gas fracking could fuel the UK for ten years say US experts"; is the headline on 11th of June 2013 Business Telegraph. Fracking involves blasting water and chemicals into the ground and extracting gas and oil trapped there (mainly gas).

The first production test well was carried out in Blackpool in 2011. It caused a series of earthquakes that were felt all around the area. The government imposed a ban on all fracking, which has since been lifted. If we ignore the headlines and the 'experts', who have a lot to gain by carrying on surveys at the taxpayers expense, the situation is not quite what is seems. There will be minor earthquakes in populated areas with unforeseen damage. It will require government subsidies to make it worthwhile economically.

There are enormous differences between the US and the UK. In the US there are acres and acres of land which can be bought up prior to commercial drilling. There are only a few inhabitants involved. A few minor earthquakes can be catered for. The US has a long history of earthquakes and the legislation to go with it. In the UK we do not.

Fracking involves a lot more government hand outs to make it worthwhile. It should be allowed in a few places well removed from the population centres when the true costs can be assessed. This is an interesting development but I cannot see it contributing more than a couple of percent to the national grid.

Renewable Energy

The remaining 9% is listed as renewable energy and 2% as others! This comes from better insulation of buildings, wind turbines, electrical generation and bio fuels. We will have a look at each of these in turn.

Wind Turbines

It is difficult get a figure for the contribution of wind turbines to the national grid. They always quote the **maximum power output** – it is a con, and the reader should be conscious of this. In optimum conditions they can be running at no more than 30 % of the wind power available. If this drops they are likely to be running at no more than 10% and, if the wind stops, they will contribute nothing. Some need to be turned off if there is too much wind which compromises the structure.

A lot of people are making a lot of money out of government subsidies and still the government wants more. There are calm days in the middle of the winter when they will contribute very little to the grid, just when we need more power. We should cut right back on these schemes to make money available for other worthwhile projects.

Local Pumped Schemes.

These require a very good flow rate of water or ideally a rise and fall of the water in a very short distance and a dam to even out the flow of water. They were once a common feature throughout the land where they were used to grind flour and power mills. We now have the means of converting any electricity to the normal grid voltage and buying back any surplus to local requirements.

The reader will probably recognise one in their locality; some being used but others have fallen into disrepair. I can think of one near me where the dam has been restored for fishing, there are still the remains of the original mill and it is ideal.

This is a sensible use of our resources with maximum demand in the winter months and minimum in summer. We should go ahead with these schemes but I doubt if they will ever contribute more than about 1% or 2% to the national grid.

Solar Panels

There are two distinct uses for solar panels; for heating and production of electricity; we will look at each one in turn:

Solar Panels for Heating

A reader who has travelled to Mediterranean countries will be familiar with solar heating panels. Some will be designed with a back up system, normally gas, for periods of high demand. This normally occurs when people are getting showered before an evening meal. It is fine for a Mediterranean country and provides an economic solution.

Israel was one of the first countries to introduce government legislation and in 1980 it passed a law requiring solar energy to be fitted on all new homes. Now, 85% of their housing is fitted with solar panels.

In this Country we do not get anywhere near Mediterranean conditions of clear blue skies in winter as well as summer. Even with a solar tracking device which will adjust for the height of the sun month by month. There is a plethora of literature out there which will tell you that even if the sky is cloudy and overcast there will still be benefits from diffuse radiation. What they fail to tell you is how much that radiation will be, compared to a clear blue sky.

Once again it is a con held together with government subsidies.

Electrical Panels

These rely on photovoltaic cells. This is an ingenious device which turns solar light directly into electricity. There are now solar tiles which do the same thing. These have the disadvantage of not being able to track the sun; once installed you just have to hope that they have been installed at an average height of the sun and, of course, facing it.

Once again it is a con held together with government subsidies. They are applicable to Mediterranean countries where they will no doubt be an economic solution to their energy problems. We should stop funding both schemes in the UK and put the money to better use elsewhere.

Hydro-Electric Power

Some countries such as Norway and Canada could use Hydro-Electric Power to fully satisfy their needs. We have nothing south of the border and some limited possibilities in Scotland.

Biomass Fuels – A Wrong usage

Under the Climate Act of 2008, the UK is 'legally bound' to reduce greenhouse gas emissions by 90% based on 1990 levels by 2050.

I sadly read an article in the PE (Professional Engineering) as recently at May 2013. The Drax, the UK's largest power station in Selby in North Yorkshire, is to be converted from conventional coal to biomass fuels and the process is well underway with the first storage tanks already installed.

They will be using some biomass produced in the UK. But the shortfall from what is available locally is nowhere near enough to satisfy a greedy power station.

Incidentally did you know that the price of logs for home consumption has risen over the last couple of years? They are burnt in the modern equivalent of the old fashioned stoves which I still have – very inefficient. The people who bought the economic stoves, on the assumption that they would be saving energy, are doing the same as Drax does. Of course resources were local with a minimum of transportation, now forest clearing could end up at the Drax power station.

I know my two sons have converted to the new economy stoves. One has a reliable source of wood at hand and can quickly go out and replace with fallen trees; all he needs is a chain saw and trailer. My other son is not quite so lucky. With the price of logs up by 80%; he is desperately seeking new supplies.

Back to Drax. They will not be making up with the shortfall in UK supplies; they are already anticipating taking the bulk of their stock from Canada. These will need transporting from source in Canada, by rail to a storage depot where they can be converted to fuel pellets. Then there will be thousands of miles of transportation cost to the UK. Then they have the unloading costs before they can be finally fitted into the storage domes at the power station. That is if everything goes to plan but unfortunately, if the plan breaks down, and the biomass fuels get wet, plans then break down. It can swell to three times its size if moisture is present and it cannot be burnt. If it comes into contact with moisture in the storage tanks it can ignite just as a haystack where the hay has not been dried thoroughly. (It could require new security arrangements for arsonists?)

This is a heavily funded government 'initiative' as is the government's 'initiative' to get rid of coal which it is currently powering some of the Drax turbines. This can soon be covered by 'renewable energy'; only politicians could have thought up anything so daft.

Methane Digesters

These have been around a long time. It was about 30 years ago when I first went on a visit to a methane digester on a pig farm. The farmer did his own research and it was before the government subsidies. When I went there he was looking for a new bit of kit which had not arrived and it was not working. My last involvement with methane digesters was in 1999 when I was given the task of designing double pipe units for a heater at a sewage station. By the time the raw sewage reaches the pumping station it has already started to decompose and needs heating up to optimise the temperature for a minimum time in the digester. The heat we used was from a water heater driven by methane gas from the methane produced. It was a bit hairy dealing with the very high viscosity of the sludge. We got the order and I was very pleased (and relieved) when it came on line and performed as expected. Sadly that ended my digester experience when the contractor I had been working for retired and sold on the business that very quickly went bust.

Any form of livestock, wild animals and human beings will give off methane (and Carbon dioxide as well) as soon as their stools are emitted. With livestock at lot depends on how they are kept. The closer they are to the digester and how much stock is kept is vital to an economic use of digesters. The products of the digester can be returned to the land as an organic fertiliser. Given the right conditions they can make a useful contribution to the electricity grid.

The main motive for sewage work stations is to stop the sewage polluting waterways. There are health issues if it is reused. The methane produced can make a useful contribution to the grid but most of it will be used in keeping the plant running.

Household waste is also a source of methane. Landfill sites are quickly covered with pipes and then a membrane fitted near the top. Later they are connected to an engine where the methane produced is a useful source of electricity for the electrical grid.

They are all very interesting and new innovations are happening all the time but I doubt if they will contribute more than 1% and 2% of the national grid needs.

Intermediate Loads

Ideally we should aim for a flat profile where supply and demand are the same. It used to be an increase in domestic consumption, whenever there was a party political broadcast when most people switched on kettles. Now the modern day equivalent is when the last act of the Eurovision Song Contest comes to an end and viewers have to wait a few minutes for the final results. Measures currently taken to even out power loads are:

Pumped Storage Hydroelectricity

This requires two dams, one at a high elevation and the other one at a low elevation with a very steep cliff in-between the two. Provided there is sufficient flow of water it will operate as a normal hydroelectric dam.

The engineers running the site anticipate the periods of peak demand; they then switch to another turbine which is used to pump from the low level dam to the high level dam. In peak demand times there is a full flow as normal.

I have seen this several times on documentaries on various channels of TV. What the viewers always ask is "why can't we build more of them". The answer is that the UK has only one suitable site at Festininiog in North Wales.

Electrical Loads

Ideally these should be charged during off peak times at night.

Pattern of Working

As industry switches to the new advanced technology; with numerically controlled machines and a robotic input, the costs increase. To justify the cost they will need to be kept running with three hour shifts including weekends. This should even out the power requirements from the loading on the grid.

The Remaining Loads

These are normally catered for by gas turbines which can be switched on immediately there is a demand for a surge in the grid load.

Transportation – Electric Vehicles

Electric powered milk floats were around long before the energy crisis or general concerns about carbon dioxide emissions. This is because they were, and continue to be, the optimum engineering solution to a very unusual specification, which includes:

(1) They only needs to cover a very limited distance which even past generations of batteries could cope with.

(2) Batteries could always be recharged 'off peak' which was ideal for the power industry who are always seeking ways to even out the electrical load, and find it economic to charge less during the night.

(3) Someone at some time will have calculated the average number of stops in a typical milk round. The stops per unit distance covered are very high compared with any other road vehicle. After each stop the float needs to reach top speed again as soon as it can. A series wound electrical motor is ideal. Any internal combustion (IC) engine would not be able to accelerate so fast, increasing the time taken, and the engine would be incredibly inefficient and have a drastically reduced life span.

Electric cars and vans have now been introduced, or are about to be introduced in many of our cities and towns. With the incredible recent developments in battery technology some delivery vans and even town centre buses may now have a sensible case for using electric propulsion. The cockeyed optimists who advocate electric cars for widespread personal transport tend to base their cases on two assumptions.

The first is that because an electric motor has a far higher efficiency than any internal combustion engine, an electric car must therefore use less energy. In reality it uses far more energy.

The energy 'tree' for an IC engine car is as follows:

Fuel production
Transportation
Fuel to mechanical energy

The energy 'tree' for an electric car is as follows:

Fuel production
Transportation
Fuel to heat energy
Heat to mechanical energy
Mechanical energy to electrical energy
Electrical energy distribution
Electrical energy to mechanical energy

At each branch of the tree there are energy losses. The magnitude of the losses at each stage will depend on the type of fuel used. For example in the IC engine tree the final stage is dependant on the sophistication of the engine and the fuel used – petrol or diesel.

The efficiency of the petrol (spark ignition) engine has now increase to well over the old norm of about 25% but it is still nowhere near the maximum of 40% for a diesel (compression ignition) engine. Also, the inherent production costs are much lower so that producing diesel fuel is more energy efficient. The reader may well ask why they are now paying more for diesel than petrol at their local garage.

The answer is an economic response to the law of supply and demand. An oil refinery is designed to break down the crude oil feedstock into a wide range of different products which may vary from propane gas to tar. Two of the most important products in the 'middle range' are petroleum and diesel. The proportions of each product are relatively fixed when the refinery is designed and built. If the demand for either of them goes up so does the price until a balance is restored.

Diesel requires less refining than petrol and is therefore more energy efficient to produce and should cost a lot less than petrol. A new grassroots plant would today be designed to produce far more diesel to reflect the change in demand. Unfortunately there are very few new plants on the horizon outside the Middle East and Asia. The UK will probably have to make do with revamping, once again, our decades old refineries. (I have worked on revamps for low sulphur, ultra low sulphur, and unleaded petrol etc.) Even revamps take time and are never ideal.

A Sensible Application of Electric Vehicles

Some of our cities are now getting very unpleasant, with noxious fumes emitted by trucks and cars. Local electric vehicles can make some difference. They should be charged at night and are not suitable for long journies.

The reader will know by now that we are not driving a zero emission car; we are simply transferring the emissions to the power stations (very uneconomically)

Other alternative means of propulsion – Hydrogen

What makes a hydrogen car possible is a device called a **fuel cell**, which converts hydrogen to electricity, giving off only heat and water as byproducts. These are already marketed in California. They require a hydrogen tank which can be filled up at specific locations.

They are not new; they have been around since the early 1900's. This of course needs very large tanks to hold the hydrogen and a source of hydrogen. The source of hydrogen can be a refinery or electrolysis of water.

They are currently used by celebrities who have unlimited money but like to be told that they are eco-friendly.

The Dearman Engine

In the 2012 February edition of the PE (Professional Engineer) it was reported that Ricardo were working with Dearman to develop a prototype engine which uses cryogenic liquids to provide power. The liquid would be either air or nitrogen (basically air without the oxygen which is currently produced for a variety of uses).

The liquid is boiled off in a confined space and the resulting high pressure gas is expanded in a cylinder to drive a crankshaft.

It is expected to be a competitor to vehicles powered by hydrogen, fuel cells and battery derived electricity. They share the common feature of zero noxious emissions at the point of use. However the overall noxious emissions released into the atmosphere and the overall efficiency will be no greater than the electric car.

Modern Cars

I have just bought a modern car; my last one was over ten years old. It cost about £10,000 pounds; a lot less than I paid for the old one; allowing for inflation a lot, lot less.

It is far more economical but it comes with gadgets I will probably never use. Every time they bring out a new car they seem to bring in more gadgets. I just wish that they would use their economy for any future cars without the gadgets. Overall the improvement in economy is staggering.

Aircraft Propulsion

These have improved too; there is far less noise, increase in payloads and more economic to run.

There is a lobby to cut down on air travel and take holidays at home. This will fail; people will demand more and more air travel. When I talk to people from June onwards the conversation quickly comes around to holidays abroad to get away from our climate, the latest bargains on the net and somewhere they repeatedly go. Some have jobs which are just above the minimum wage but they look forward to their holiday in the sun.

They can extend Heathrow if they like but no more in the South East despite Boris's objections. New airports should be made available to the rest of the UK, particularly long haul flights e.g. Birmingham.

Bio-Fuels – Hopefully the Correct Usage.

We have already looked at one bio-fuel in the section on main line generation. Bio-fuels cover a wide range of options: these are alternative methods to propulsion, many of which are now being used.

Bio-fuels originate in living organisms and the theory is that what is taken from the planet is eventually returned to the planet which produces a carbon free balance. Some of them have been around for a long time but others are quite new; I will look at each one in turn:

Bio ethanol

Bio ethanol is an alcohol which is produced by fermentation. The reader will be familiar with a similar process which produces methyl alcohol – the one that we drink. During the fermentation process to produce the one which we drink air should be excluded otherwise we will produce some ethanol as well (home brewers will be familiar with this).

A few years ago there was said to be a 'wine lake' due to over production of wine in the EU. This was converted from methyl alcohol to ethanol in a plant specially designed for this purpose so that it could be used as a fuel. There are people in the EU and elsewhere who would drink it but they could not afford the inflated price – not a very good example of sustainability.

Brazil is the world's largest producer of ethanol. It grew up there because of the amount of sugar they produced. They produce sugar cane and when the last of the sugar has been extracted the remains are ideal for fermentation into ethanol.

Flex Fuel Vehicles

These were introduced about 2003 and can run on pure ethane or a blended fuel which is gasoline blended with a 25% mixture of ethanol. More than 90% of new cars sold in Brazil are now flex fuel vehicles.

They still use sugar cane but this is nowhere near enough to satisfy their requirements for fermentation. They now use all sorts of organic materials and continue experimenting to find the most suitable.

These are specially designed engines and the reader could not take their car to Brazil. One downer of flex fuel vehicles is that ethanol has about half the calorific value of conventional gasoline. This means that the tanks need to be twice as large to cover the mileage and the source to the pumping stations needs to be double capacity. Brazil is far less dependant on foreign oil prices. Unfortunately this is no remedy for the UK's situation.

Biodiesel

Biodiesel is made from vegetable oils and animal fats; mainly the former. The UK is currently undergoing a transformation of its countryside with more and more acreage growing rapeseed for Biodiesel fuels.

Elsewhere they are burning a lot of pristine rainforests to plant palm oil trees which can be used for the same thing. In 2013 we had the familiar sight in Singapore of the population wearing 'gas masks' when there was no wind. The windless period coincides with a dry season in Indonesia and is ideal for burning. That part of Indonesia is just across the Malaccan Straights and it can be seen from the Malaysian peninsular and Singapore where it narrows at the southernmost tip.

The Indonesians do not have the time to harvest the timber there; it is just slash and burn before the rainy season starts and they can plant the palm oil trees which will replace them.

The largest market for palm oil is the EU. Palm oil and rapeseed oil is added to conventional diesel. It has the added bonus of reducing the levels of particulates in a conventional diesel and improving lubrication. It eliminates the black cloud that is usually associated with diesels exhausts and the emissions which can cause breathing problems.

Ethanol to Increase Octane Number

In the UK and elsewhere in the EU ethanol can be used to increase the octane number thus raising the compression ratio which can be used which can improve the engine efficiency. We can not go too far with this unless we have a period of dual pumps at filling stations when older models would suffer from knock as the compression ratios increase.

Today

Bio fuels make up about 3% of transformation fuels in the UK. This will increase to about 7% by 2030.

Domestic Heating Loads

We live in a temperate climate and have no need for air conditioning in summer so this basically comes down to heating in winter. As we get older we tend to feel the cold more than when we were young.

As a new build there is the choice of gas (bottled in rural areas) and electricity (always needed to turn on the gas). For district heating schemes they should have a back up generator if the electricity fails. For most of us we have no choice.

Decreasing losses are now something to which the government is heavily committed. The losses consist of roof losses, floor losses, window losses, losses through the building structure and ventilation losses. Over 40 years ago when I first started teaching window losses I checked on what was being done in some Scandinavian countries. There they had legislation, Those windows that could not be opened were triple glazed and windows that could be opened were double glazed. Only now have the government done something similar by insisting that all replacement windows should be double glazed or secondary glazed.

Floor losses can be catered for by fitting a thick underlay under carpeting but if you have tiled or wood block floorings this should have been fitted before it went down and it is expensive to retro-fit.

One of the main losses is through the roof. The current government legislation is for a minimum of 100 mm (8 inches) of insulation; there are pitfalls to this which should be pointed out during a preliminary survey. The attic should be well ventilated to prevent condensation and any of the now dated cold water tanks could freeze in winter. Care should also be taken to ensure that no power cables are directly under the insulation without precautions, so that the heat produced by the power cables can escape.

All new central heating boilers should be fitted with thermostatic control valves, an excellent idea. People fitting them will also claim that they are condensing boilers. Only when they start up and shut down will they be operating in a condensing mode. The exhaust gas needs to be cooled below the dew point (about 50°C) for condensation to take place. The exception to this is where they are under floor or over floor heating fitted. These operate at about 25°C and are supplied with heating at about 35°C in which case they will be operating in the condensing mode all the time.

Losses through the building structure are not without their problems. If a cavity wall is fitted without the bricklayer depositing a lot of mortar on the tie bars in-between the layers of bricks (far too often) it will ventilate fine until a cavity wall is installed. Then it becomes a 'cold bridge'. A lot of people have had cavity walls insulated in the summer months, only to find that they have damp problems in the winter on their internal walls.

I think that the government has reacted to create so many 'experts' on crash courses when they do not have a sound background. Then of course there are the people who will cash in on drumming up 'experts' who work for a fee. Sometimes we get as much as three phone calls a week to ask if we have cavity insulation installed; only to be told that we have solid brick walls that date back to before cavity filled walls existed.

Despite some excesses I think that the government is now doing a good job of keeping domestic energy losses to a minimum.

Conclusions

(1)   We should support research and development into a wide range of energy projects, sharing these costs with other countries whenever possible for the larger projects. There should be no cut backs in this field; we should **spend more.**

(2)   Nuclear power is the only proven option available at the moment for supplying an efficient, carbon dioxide free base electrical load. We should extend the life of existing power stations wherever possible and build new ones **now**, although it may already be too late.

(3)   Because of the long lead time for any nuclear build or revamp we must accept that in the **short term** we need to keep conventional coal fired stations operating, ideally using British coal – we have reserves which could last for hundreds of years. Irresponsible politicians have set unrealistic targets for reducing carbon dioxide emissions.

(4)   Gas is the most flexible fuel available to us. Apart from widespread domestic use it is currently used by many industries. It is the ideal fuel for combined heat and power plants – large and small – which should be increased. It is also used in gas turbines in main power stations to provide peak lopping loads. With politically sensitive supplies it should **not** be squandered by using it to provide base loads in main power stations.

(5) We should stop wasting money through **artificial subsidies** on projects which will never provide either a reliable base load or a peak lopping load. **Wind power and solar power** are currently the main culprits. Cutting back on the money currently being spent on subsidies for these should balance the books and provide finance for other areas.

For the Future

Nuclear fission should not be compared with nuclear fusion. Nuclear fission is the bringing together of uranium so that criticality is reached where the rate of decay of uranium is sufficient to produce energy in the form of neutrons and photons. The products produced are not the same as the original uranium. This is a conventional nuclear power station as discussed above.

Fusion is the bringing together of deuterium and tritium in a critical mass sufficient to produce energy. The products are water and helium. Two atoms of water fuse together to produce one atom of helium and the energy released obeys the law of $e = m \times c^2$ where c is the velocity of light in a vacuum. The velocity of light is enormous as is the energy produced.

One in every 64 molecule of water is deuterium and it is only about 11% denser and mixes freely with other water molecules. The reader will have consumed more than enough deuterium to keep them and thousands around them supplied with energy in a fusion process.

Helium is an inert gas second only to hydrogen in density. It has a molecular mass of about 4 compared with hydrogen about 2. The reader will be aware of the uses for helium; hot air balloons, welding and cryogenics.

The sun is powered by fusion and emits enormous amounts of helium. Ever since we tested the first hydrogen bomb we know mankind can produce the same thing. The physics is there; we just have to control it. In the past whenever the physics have been proven it has not been too far behind for engineers to do the rest. What is it that up to now has prevented us taking advantage of unlimited power with no environmental impacts?

Temperature – up till now scientists have only been able to maintain fusion for fractions of a second. To do this they use a Large Hadron Collider (LHC) which spans the Franco-Swiss boarder and uses superconducting magnets to maintain fusion. It is a start, but we still have a long way to go. I will never see a solution in my lifetime but possibly my grandchildren will see it. Until then it will remain the 'holy grail' of cheap abundant electricity.

THE WATER CRISIS

I am writing this section in the spring of 2012. In the area where I live we have just had a record dry month in March followed by a record wet month in April. Councils have embarrassingly high stocks of grit for de-icing the roads following a very mild winter; after running out of grit during the previous cold winter. England is one of the few countries where the weather is a regular topic of conversation throughout the year. In other countries it is more likely to be a seasonal topic and limited to 'when will the monsoon rains start' or 'when will the mistral start to blow'.

The mild winter was also an unusually dry one, particularly in the South East where it had followed a year of below average rainfall. In March the hot weather topic was hosepipe bans and restrictions on the use of water. East Anglia had already imposed a ban and other regions had fixed dates for a ban to start. The measures planned to follow the hosepipe bans would have had far reaching effects for the public, agriculture and the economy.

By the end of April bans had been postponed and by mid summer the reservoirs in the South East were full and the hot topic of conversation was the floods. Many parts of the country had storms where up to 50 mm (2 inches) of rain fell in a few hours. In the South East this was far more than their norm for a month. I measured a full two inches which fell in less than two hours on my rain gauge. One of my sons, who lives about 15 miles away in Shropshire, was devastated when a section of his home was washed away. When he heard about it at work he had to ditch his car and walk the last mile to reach his family who were all at home when the flood had hit them. Fortunately no one was hurt. I will never forget what I saw when I arrived later that day.

The hosepipe crisis had been followed by the wettest summer ever with many rainfall records being broken. The UK was not the only country to be affected by a small deviation in the Gulf Stream but this chapter is not the right one to discuss it; now I will limit it to a problem I can remember first discussing a long time ago when I was a student – the need for a national water grid.

I had the following article published in the PE (Professional Engineering), the magazine of the IMechE. (Institution of Mechanical Engineers)

A Sensible 'Wind turbine' Application?

A wind turbine in the right place, servicing the right load, often provides an economic solution to a problem. The folly of trying to provide a significant proportion of the electrical load on our national grid using wind turbine power has been exposed many times by readers.

Another problem which always crops up whenever there is a spell of reasonable weather is the water shortage in the South East which will get progressively worse as that area expands at the expense of the rest of the country. One of the latest ways to overcome this problem is a desalination plant designed to occasionally produce very expensive water – a triumph for technology or stupidity?

A 'national' grid system for water distribution was recently suggested by Scottish 'politicians' who proposed selling their excess of water to the South East. The idea was quickly dismissed by English 'politicians' as too costly because of the pumping costs. (The ideal of a grid system for water is not new; it must have been around almost as long as I have.)

The idea then occurred to me, what about a 'national/international' grid system for water powered by wind turbines? The main problems with producing electrical power from wind turbines are the variable load, electrical transmission losses and the difficulties in storing electricity. These are far easier to overcome with a water grid system.

The wind turbines could be directly coupled to the pumps on some sites and use electrical power from wind turbines on adjacent hills in others. There are obvious storage points at many locations in the form of existing reservoirs. There is also a much less obvious and much larger storage system – the water table of the London basin. A lot of

London's water is extracted from bore holes and the progressive lowering of the water table as a result is another matter for concern.

At one extreme, with no wind (unlikely for every pumping station), there would be no flow and water would be taken from the reservoirs as it is now. At the other extreme when there was full power from the wind turbines water would flow along the grid and, as the reservoirs approached their capacity, extraction from boreholes would cease and the water table could be replenished.

I have used the term 'politician' in the very general sense to include advisers and administrators of the various government and utility organisations involved.

Bill Watson Staffordshire – Fellow

Today

Nothing has changed my mind since I wrote that article. It has even come to my notice that there is a natural contour line stretching from London to the far north, Durham, Cumbria and then into Scotland where there will never be any shortages of water. The grid could be buried on some stretches and open water at others, a canal. All that is needed is a few wind turbines to keep it going. There should be no environmental issues; most people would welcome a canal passing through their land, unlike a high speed train.

There are precedents to ambitious water projects in the UK; the finest one is the Elan Valley Dam which was designed just before 1900. It involved building a 73 mile long tunnel from the source of the fresh water in Wales to Birmingham. It was the idea of James Mansergh, a man of real vision as to what could be done with the equipment he had available. It involved crossing the river Wye on an aqueduct, some tunnelling, and work was commenced on the first part of the project in 1896.

It is a natural convection system and the water travels at less than 2 miles per hour so that the total time it takes from the valleys to Birmingham is one and a half days. It was over budget but it took less than ten years to build. When it was finally switched on, nothing happened. Despite his assurance that it would take time, Mansergh originally did a 'runner'; later the next day water started to flow, and he emerged as a genius.

It served Birmingham well for many years and led to a rapid growth in population in Birmingham and the subsequent trades that went with it. Now Birmingham has new supplies of water but the old Elan is still being used to this day.

With modern equipment and a few wind-powered turbines we could solve the water crisis. We still have engineers with vision who can see the future.

What is left now is for politicians to see beyond the next election. Now that the water companies have been split up there are a few inadequate schemes, like a short run from the Severn estuary to feed the headwaters of the Thames. This is no substitute for a proper national grid which would serve the county well into the future and provide a much needed boost for the construction companies.

NATIONAL HEALTH SERVICE (NHS)

The NHS was set up by the first Labour government after the Second World War. I can just recall the way it used to be before then when people had to pay. I was a sickly child and I suppose I built up my fair share of debts. Many years later I learned that I had a sister who was misdiagnosed as a child when she was suffering with pneumonia.

Now we are in a situation when the National Health Service is criticised for just about everything. 'Not fit for purpose', 'failing to provide', shortage of this and that and failure to provide cover for certain geographical areas. The situation is not helped by the number of 'soaps' where there is always an emergency and they are trying hard to stay within the system.

The NHS is changing to keep up with innovations. I remember my son had an appendix operation. He had key-hole surgery and was out the next day doing some light painting. I remember having the same thing when key-hole was unknown and I spent a week recuperating in hospital. I recently spent some time having an operation for a double hernia. The same thing, I was out within about four hours after the operation – no need for a hospital bed.

It is easy to criticise but some of the regulations are as a result of the media in hot pursuit for a story – such as 'he cut off the wrong leg'. Now I have a routine blood test and every time I have to go through date of birth, postcode etc even though the receptionist has the card in front of her and I know her quite well by now. Overall I and my family have had very satisfactory treatment on the NHS.

A dangerous situation

One very dangerous situation has cropped up and that is to judge surgeons on their failures rates. I have just composed three fictitious surgeons to bring out this point.

	Mr N O Risk	Mr C Agy	Mr C H Allenge
Operations	110	100	90
Deaths	0	1	10

The media might classify Mr N O Risk as being ideal and Mr C H Allenge as someone who should be forced into retirement or worse. A detailed analysis of the operations showed that the first two surgeons with the impressive statistics had declined to operate on patients where there was a high risk of death because of the complexity and the uncertainty of the procedures involved. Mr C H Allenge's patients included 35 that Mr N O Risk had declined to operate on and 15 that Mr C Agy had declined to operate on. (This left 50% of Mr C H Allenge work that was routine and something that the others could have done which left 50% of his work which was not routine and could have resulted in death to a patient.)

The reader should think carefully if they require a surgeon, (not that many of course have a choice).

Hospital Environment

People who are admitted to hospital are ill; otherwise they would not be admitted. My father and mother both died in hospital. The overall death rate is a function of what the hospital has to offer.

I remember the Legionnaires crisis because a number of my ex students were involved. It was the atmospheric cooling towers which were the culprit. They had managed to leak into the main air conditioning system. If this had happened with a normal fit population many of them would not have noticed. Others might have experienced a few muscle aches and loss of appetite. However in a hospital environment people are being treated with all sorts of problems and it can rapidly develop into pneumonia. This is what happened and a lot of people died as a result. Nowadays there are very strict rules governing the temperature of the water and cleaning of all surfaces from which a problem may occur.

This is a dramatic incident but there will always be minor ones from visitors and staff alike. Hospital and Doctor's surgeries are unhealthy environments and it is best to stay clear of them whenever possible. As far as hospitals are concerned many people die there and that is a fact of life.

Training of NHS staff.

It is interesting that the government's 'new' initiative on training is to go straight into a job instead of going on to academic training with all the debts involved. Doctors' qualifications are never mentioned. This is the way it was many years ago but the exception is doctors, just as it always was. The doctors' qualification is always a misnomer because it involves doing some original work to take a PhD. A lot of a doctor's' work is taken up as practical training, particularly towards the end when they are regarded as cheap labour.

The powerful BMA has a lot to do with this but they also should be persuaded to change to keep up with the times. A nurse, midwife and others should be allowed to train and reach the ultimate of their profession i.e. achieve doctor status. They must of course demonstrate the necessary academic standards.

I am fully aware that nurses now have degree status of entry. (I can remember when there were no academic standards to train as a nurse!) Although things have changed nurses will ultimately have to answer to a doctor who is in charge of the medical profession. The majority of nurses will be happy to carry on in their present position but there will be some who are not.

There may be a series of credits to achieve this but ultimately they will have to pass the same academic standards. A nurse could opt for the same courses as they do now but some of them could accept the challenge of sitting the same exams as the medical student. It would of course take longer but they will be getting paid during their training. This would set the medical profession on the same path as the other professions. It might take as long as, say, fifteen years to achieve this but who knows what hidden talents there exist and could benefit us all.

The care of the elderly and terminally ill.

We all know that we will have to face the inevitable and die. Unfortunately there are many religious organisations that will not let us go. God gave life and it is up to him when he chooses to take it away. The suffering brigade does not accept that. This causes heartbreak to the individual and their loved ones. If they stick to that, (and if it is what the individual wants) they should be free to have it but they should not be allowed to influence the rest of us.

On Sunday, 20 June 2010 I wrote a letter to a Dr Martin. (He admitted helping patients to die knowing that he could face criminal charges but wished to open a debate on euthanasia.)

Dear Dr Martin,

I have read sufficient about your case to appreciate the situation you now find yourself in. You will no doubt be receiving a lot of negative mail from the 'sanctity of existence and the virtues of suffering' brigade. I hope you receive many more from people like me who understand and appreciate how you have helped both individuals and society during your career.

I was fortunate enough to be involved with a like minded consultant when it came to the situation when my late father had reached the point of no return to a reasonable life. If I am ever in that position myself I have already told my children that I would like to be remembered for the things that I have achieved during my life and not as a helpless human cabbage. It is an unfortunate fact of life that our last memories of anyone are often the most vivid.

If there is any way that I can help, such as being a positive witness to your claim that your attitudes to helping people are more widespread than many people think, please contact me.

I hope that the increasingly rare commodity, common sense, prevails and you can be left in peace to enjoy your retirement.

I am sure that there are many other people who think like me on this issue and I hope that some of them will take the trouble to let you know.

Bill Watson

Paul Blomfield the Labour MP

More recently I read a report from parliament by Paul Blomfield the Labour MP for Sheffield Central.

In April 2012 Paul Blomfield had total quiet in the usually boisterous House of Commons when he called for a change in the law on assisted suicide. He told the house about his father Henry who was an ex-RAF pilot. He had reached the age of 87 and had terminal cancer. To avoid his family being involved he took his own life whilst he was still able to do so. To save himself from a lingering and degrading death he gassed himself using the car exhaust in his garage.

Paul said that he knew he would have preferred to end his own life among friends than alone in a smoke-filled garage. He would also have had the choice of waiting a little longer if the law had been different. As it was he waited until one of his better days and took what he probably thought would be his last chance.

Euthanasia twins - nothing to live for.

This concerns a case which took place in Belgium in January 2013 where euthanasia is allowed, provided that the patient's wishes are clear when they visit a doctor who then terminates their lives with a lethal injection.

The twins spent most of their time working as cobblers, shared the same house and were inseparable. They could communicate only by using a special sign language known only to themselves and immediate family. Mark and Eddy Verbessem had been born deaf and with a genetical form of glaucoma which could make one of them blind as well; so they could not communicate.

They made the decision that they would go together rather than face a life of dependency where they could no longer work. They must have had some religious beliefs because "together with my parents" was one thing they were looking forward to in the afterlife; before they bid their last goodbyes and the injection took a hold. They were only 45 when they died.

Now in the UK

Now in the UK there is utter confusion. It is not too bad for those in the South East who have the time and money to spend in getting loved ones there to volunteer to go to a euthanasia clinic abroad. Even then they have to choose the right moment to end their lives.

I would like to see terminally ill patients given the same choice as those in certain European countries. The euthanasia clinics have flourished because of the demand from abroad. In most cases they die in dignity in their own homes where they can see their loved ones. Most Physicians are atheists and are readily agreeable to this practice.

Hospices abroad.

In Germany a hospice is something you never come out of. It is meant for the terminally ill and when they are admitted they know that. In between they are treated with respect and dignity until the dosage of morphine is increased and they can die peacefully in their sleep.

Care Homes, Hospices and Hospitals

I pay regular visits to a care home. It is ideal. The residents can cook their own meals or go down to a service centre when they wish. The lady I visit is over 90 and is still good company (although she is starting to get a bit repetitive in what she says). She recognises everyone and can still remember the last time I called

Other centres are not ideal. The patients suffer the dreaded Alzheimer's disease. They can remember well for a short while and then there is nothing. Many famous names are included in this list and many of them would like to make the decision as to when they would choose to die.

Others do not recognise any one at all and have to be force fed. This can go one for a long time – what is the point of it? It ties up valuable staff time and it means that we have to build another home and more staff has to be provided to staff it.

The legal argument against this is that some relatives may be persuaded to 'jump the gun' where an inheritance is involved. I think that there are a few who might do this and I would leave it to their conscience. Making a legal decision for the very few compared to the majority does not make sense and I would do away with the legal bit.

There are a lot of people out there who no longer have anything to offer and they should be allowed to die with dignity and compassion.

I have told my children that if I ever reach the state where I cannot be critical of everyday events just as I am doing now, it is time to go. I would like to be remembered for what I achieved in life rather than as a doddering old fool who went on too long. I hope that this country will have come to its senses by then and I have a freedom of choice.

Test tube baby

In vitro fertilisation (IVF) is a process during which a woman's ova are removed and fertilised in a laboratory using sperm from the father. The fertilised egg is then inserted into the woman's uterus. The first successful birth was Louise Brown in 1978. Robert G Edwards who developed this treatment was awarded the Nobel Prize in Physiology or Medicine in 2010.

A lot has happened since then. The woman no longer has to receive sperm from the husband or partner; it can be a sperm donor. This is ideal when the husband has a genetic defect which can be passed on to the child.

It is generally recognised that the ideal age for IVF is a woman in her mid thirties. It is now possible for a mother to have the fertilized eggs frozen for a later date when she is ready to have a child. This can resort to all sorts of legal issues if she no longer has the same partner.

One problem with IVF is that it can give rise to multiple births. Some practitioners ensure that only one birth is possible; others do not (It does not prevent the remote possibility of identical twins.)

Now we have another scenario where the child conceived may have more than one biological mother. Not all the eggs are fertilised in a laboratory; some of it is inserted into a surrogate mother. The donor will thus have some input for the subsequent child. Where this prevents a genetic defect in the child's mother being a problem this is to be a good thing. (The legal aspect is another matter; if the donor decides she wants to keep the child.)

Any form of IVF is costly to the NHS. The complexity is dependant on the treatment required. We now have a situation where women are **'demanding'** NHS treatment no matter what the cost.

There is no way that any woman's **'demands'** can be at the expense of the other NHS treatment in other fields. If they satisfy the criteria in my chapter on eugenics they can well afford to pay.

An underlying theme in this book is that we need to limit our population. Ideally it should be decreased. How else can we be hypocritical and ask the world to do the same. Already we have women **'demanding'** IVF who are now on state benefits.

SPORT

I have personally sampled a wide variety of sports at some time in my life including rugby union, football, cricket, water polo, swimming, basketball, tennis, table tennis, badminton, squash, running, jumping, javelin and discus throwing, boxing, judo, beach and gym volleyball, golf, sailing, Olympic weightlifting and Power weightlifting.

I was introduced to many of the above activities at school where sport was an important part of the curriculum and compulsory. I cannot recall anyone not taking part but sadly very few of today's children have the same opportunities.

I had some ability with the throwing events and once even had a go with the hammer at a university sports day. (A bit dangerous and stupid because I had never picked one up before 'having a go'.) My limited successes at school were in swimming, where I won a few medals, and water polo, once being captain when I was the youngest member of the squad. At university I took part in the first ever British University Olympic weightlifting competition in Sheffield. That first year the standards were generally very low and although I did not get a medal I still have a piece of paper to show that I was the runner up in the mid-heavyweight division.

Other sports I took up much later in life. I was over 50 when I first tried badminton. I was working in the Netherlands at the time and a group of us used to go straight from work. It was good fun and I enjoyed it but the only one I ever managed to beat was a one eyed cockney called Pete (and that was only when I repeatedly hit the shuttlecock into his blind side of the court).

Definition of a Sport

An individual or group activity pursued for exercise or pleasure often involving the testing of physical capabilities and taking the form of competitive games such as football.

The origins of the Olympic Games

The original Olympic Games were held at Olympia in Greece in 776 BC. The only participants were from states in the immediate area. A four year cycle was established and the events were limited to running, throwing, fighting and equestrian. They lasted for over a millennium before finally petering out after Greece became part of the Roman Empire.

They were revived in Athens in 1896 and have continued ever since except for the interruptions caused by major wars. They have progressively developed and undergone many changes since then. Athens is now just one of the worldwide cities which compete to hold them. It is arguable whether all the participants in the original Olympic Games would be described as amateurs but the modern version was intended to be strictly an amateur competition.

2012 Olympic Games

In 1986 the International Olympic Committee (IOC) changed its charter to allow "all the world's great athletes" to compete in the Olympic Games.

There is no doubt that this was long overdue, I have never been to the Olympics but like the majority I sit glued to the television for the duration of the games. There are minority sports which fascinate me and I like to know the pros and cons of the rules. However I will very seldom see the minority sports again until the next Olympics.

Every year there are more and more sports included and in the 2012 Games I thought it farcical that so many team games were included. It is supposed to be "all the world's great athletes" but was the football included in this? I have never seen so many rules invented to make sure that it was not. Footballers have their own competitions with a world cup once every four years and a European cup once every four years sandwiched in-between. They never have to go more that two years without a major competition. (The European cup has the same set up with the same faces as the world cup except that some S American countries are excluded.) Then there is the African cup, the America cup etc. If you ask any football fan to name the finalists of the last few World and European cups they could name them, but will have already forgotten the names of the Olympic finalists.

When sports have their own cup, they should not be a part of the Olympic Games. Tennis is another one to have Grand Slam tournaments every year (Australian, US, French and Wimbledon) played over five sets (why should women get away with three sets when they demand equal payments!). Many tennis players did not even bother to take part in 2012 and preferred the kudos of a 'grand slam' competition. Admittedly the UK did rather well and I watched every minute of it, but that is no excuse.

The sheer weight of numbers at the London Olympics should be cut by about a third. Otherwise few Cities will be able to afford the accommodation to make it worth their while – could Greece, the home of the Olympics, now afford it?

Who Benefited from 2012?

The catch phrase is 'we all did' but the rider is 'some more than others'. Provided you could save up a few days holiday entitlement, or in my case suspend my writing, we could watch what we wanted on television. Everyone I know was fascinated by some aspect of the games.

Then there was the build up; with the Olympic torch run taking in most major cities and a few villages as well. But I still have to meet anyone who took time off to personally attend to any of the events in London.

We all paid through our taxes and before there was some talk about having the games outside London – Birmingham, Manchester, Leeds and Liverpool, with a multi-city games. That was soon scotched and it had to be in London.

There is no doubt that the individual who will benefit most from the London Olympics will be its Mayor, Boris Johnson. He will 'modestly' take some credit for all the new facilities and improved infrastructure in the capital which will enhance his CV for the day he makes his bid to become prime minister.

He also has a rival for future prime minister, Sebastian Coe who is a fully paid up member of the Tory party. He can also claim some credit for what has been done in London. When asked recently about the legacy of the 2012 games, it was all to do with London.

London now has a new tube line connecting the East End of London to what used to be a dilapidated rundown area and is now an up-market site. They have created new stadia and they are still arguing about how to reuse them – a new football stadium?

Boris Johnston now wants another London airport situated on reclaimed land on the Isle of Grain in East London. Sebastian Coe would settle for another runway at Heathrow. Already Luton airport has now become North London airport.

But what of the rest of us who still reside 'North of the Watford Gap'. We are still the majority of the population in the UK. What has the aftermath of 2012 done for us? I continually hear our local television (Midlands Today) giving positive answers to this question. One is that a Midland company was given the contract to produce the Olympic Torch. They seem to be doing well but they only employ a very small workforce.

It truly was the **London** Olympic Games and I look forward to the next Olympics in Rio when I will do the same as I did this time and watch it on TV.

DEFENCE & WAR

For many years after World War 2 the UK continued to have a place at the top table in world affairs. We had an Empire which was soon to become a Commonwealth. However we were lumbered with war debts, the last of which was repaid to the USA in 2011.

We continued to provide an Army in Germany well after it was needed. This drained our resources when others were building infrastructure.

Now we should accept that we are no longer a 'top player' in world affairs. There are debates about whether we should give up our nuclear 'deterrent' or buy into the latest nuclear upgrades offered by the USA. It will be expensive to accept the USA offer at a time when we need to cut back on our expenditure. We should look carefully to see if there is any other option open to us.

The nuclear deterrence we have now is no longer the sophisticated devices possessed by our 'enemies' who have smart bombs and missiles.

Let us look at these 'enemies' and see what happens in practice. There are 'rogue states' such as North Korea. They know that they would never use them except as a negotiating tool to ensure that the USA would not attack them. (If they gave up their nuclear option what would they have left to negotiate with the USA). If they did use them they would be obliterated by the USA. Despite their rhetoric and postures they would not want that.

Then there is Iran who may well have nuclear ambitions and has some missiles to deliver them. As soon as they have that ability it would be snuffed out by Israel and the USA.

Our Real 'Enemies'.

I can think of only one – Argentina. We now have a lot more cover there than the last Falklands war, when we surrendered the territory with minimum loss of life to the local population. Then came the bloody battle, to regain control of the Falklands. The military are now agreed that we do not have the facilities to mount such at task force again. Our troops and aircraft could hang on a lot longer than the first time that Argentina attacked but they would eventually be overrun.

It is no good looking to the USA for help; they would be looking at their own interests. I think that we should update our existing nuclear capability to keep it going for a little bit longer. It would not mean any smart bombs and missiles – just providing a cover in the southern oceans with one nuclear submarine. At the first sign of an Argentine attack it would be there before our limited troops could be overwhelmed. All it would need would be a warning that their airbases would be attacked. They would be told that all aircraft should be grounded and sufficient time allowed for civilian and military personnel to leave the area before the 'unthinkable' took place.

Argentine should be made aware of the possibility of a future attack on the Falklands and deterrence has worked yet again.

The Falkland's are determined to stay under UK's influence and with it comes a place at the top table for exploiting the Southern Hemispheres riches. It has already been proven that there is oil there, fishing grounds and a tourist industry. It also grants us a place at the top table when it comes to exploiting Antarctica.

Argentine

We should act now before it is too late. Already they have a Pope who is on their side. We know how unpredictable Argentine politics can be. A cry for 'freedom' of the Malvinas could well be answered with a new war.

Only if we counter this attack with a nuclear submarine can this threat be eliminated. Hopefully there will be sufficient time for a long lasting solution to the Falklands to be reached. They can jointly exploit the resources in the area and the Falklands could be under UK control.

A Political Compromise

In July 2013 the first of the Royal Navy's nuclear powered hunter-killer submarines became operational after years of delays (including running aground in sea trials off Scotland.) Seven are planned and there are three more in various stages of production. They cost £1 billion each; far less than buying into the American nuclear/nuclear deterrent. They carry no nuclear weapons but other than that they are equipped with all the latest technology which will last the county for decades.

They can travel from Antarctica to the Arctic submerged, without ever surfacing to a normal submarine's periscope depth. They have no periscope; they can 'see' what is going on above them while staying undetected.

They carry two missiles, one the Spearfish and the other the Tomahawk. They can fire their missiles fully submerged or on the surface. The Tomahawk missile can be reprogrammed to change direction in mid-flight.

They already have nuclear safe-guards to protect their main engines. They could carry just two nuclear warheads. They can be short-range missiles with a range of say 1,000 kilometres and they do not have to be sophisticated to deal with the Argentine threat.

This should be done now before we dismantle our current nuclear deterrent. We can still satisfy our demands from our 'allies' but with the proviso that we will keep one hunter-killer submarine close to the Falkland Islands patrolling the southern ocean.

We could save ourselves billions of pounds with this strategy. Otherwise I see no future in a nuclear deterrent and we should give them up as an example to others.

Other Books by the Same Author

Mechanical Services for Buildings
T D Eastop & W E Watson
Longman Scientific & Technical 1992

Thermal Design of Shell & Tube Heat Exchangers
Bill Watson
Shell & Tube Consultancy & Publications Ltd (satcap) 2009

A Different View of the Camino de Santiago
Bill Watson
Fast-Print Publishing 2011